Why What We Use as Money Matters

An Economic and Philosophical Treatise

DAVID MINT

Copyright © 2013 The Wilcox Trading Company

All rights reserved.

ISBN: 1493587447
ISBN-13: 978-1493587445

Cover design by David Mint at WDesign

Adaptation of a photograph of the Urbari Oasis in the Fezzan region of Southwestern Libya by Sfivat, May 17, 2005.

DEDICATION

This book is dedicated to Dani, Pau, and all future generations who will benefit and build upon its insights. It has been written so that they may better understand the world in which they live, and that they, armed with this understanding, may live out their days in peace and liberty while securing the same blessings for their posterity.

> *"The time has come," the Walrus said,*
> *"To talk of many things:*
> *Of shoes–and ships–and sealing-wax–*
> *Of cabbages–and kings–*
> *And why the sea is boiling hot–*
> *And whether pigs have wings."*

- Lines from 'The Walrus and the Carpenter', a poem recited by the characters Tweedledum and Tweedledee in Lewis Carroll's *Through the Looking-Glass* (popularly known as "Alice in Wonderland").

CONTENTS

	Acknowledgments	i
Foreword	The Calling	1
Prologue	The Subtle Change from Principles to Rules	3
Volume I	What is Truth? On the Nature of Empire	19
Volume II	What is Money? A Quest To Answer The Question of The Ages	77
Volume III	Of Money and Metals: The Operation of a Free Money Supply Explained	97
Volume IV	Atheism With Regards to Government: Anarchy as an Ultimate Given	139

Volume V	Natural Law and The Theory of Economic System Fluidity: Marx and Rand Together in Perfect Harmony	177
Volume VI	Pacioli's Gift or Bernanke's Curse? How Mankind's Greatest Innovation Has Enabled Its Greatest Catastrophe	237
Volume VII	To Build Up the Land: Thoughts on Mankind's Uneasy Intercourse With Nature	295
Epilogue	Eschatology and Money: A Brief Look at What is To Come	361
Afterword	The Charge	382
	Interior Cover Credits	384
	About the Author	387

ACKNOWLEDGMENTS

First and foremost, we wish thank to the Living God for giving us life and allowing us to encounter the answers to many of life's burning questions. We would also like to thank our wife, children, parents, and extended family who have supported us during this project in innumerable ways, from providing challenging questions to simply listening to us as we processed the many and varied themes explored in these volumes.

We are also indebted to the many writers, teachers, philosophers, and champions of the ideas that these volumes borrow from and build upon. While the champions of these ideas are many, those that have had the greatest impact upon these volumes are Jesus of Nazareth, Bill Bonner, Jason Hommel, Bettie Mitchell, Ludwig Von Mises, Ron Paul, and Adin Ballou. These volumes and indeed all of humanity are indebted to the various expressions of the above-mentioned individuals' passion for truth.

Finally, we are indebted to all individuals who, despite overwhelming odds, have kept the flame of real freedom burning throughout history, no matter what the cost. It is our hope that these volumes may honor their sacrifices by lighting the torch of freedom for many generations to come and inspiring those same generations to go and do likewise.

FOREWORD: THE CALLING

Owen Meany had a calling. The hero in John Irving's 1989 New York Times bestseller *A Prayer for Owen Meany* which was later loosely adapted to the feature length film *Simon Birch*, believed himself to be God's instrument in an unswerving and often shocking manner. Owen Meany's calling was as clear to him as it was confusing, for while he could see the end result, he could not foresee nor fully understand the varied circumstances which guided him to his encounter with destiny.

We believe that, like the fictional Owen Meany, every human being that is alive or has ever lived has a calling, something specific that is to be done in this world that only they and they alone can accomplish. The task may be ignored, but it cannot be delegated. It may require the collaboration of many to accomplish, but the burden and drive to complete the task rests with one individual.

If the task does not get done, it does not get done, and the world will be all the worse off for it.

On the other hand, if it is accomplished, all the host of heaven will applaud, for every calling that is recognized and pursued is not simply another task to be completed, it is an indispensible stitch in the fabric of what may be if only all of humanity would accept the call to a higher purpose that, far from being reserved for the exceptional, is the birthright of every human.

The following nine volumes are our calling. Taken individually, they are a winding exploration of philosophy, monetary theory, economics, dual entry accounting, climate change, and eschatology. Taken together, they are a treatise on political economy of such gravity and importance that, if fully understood by even one person among a million, will bring the activities of mankind into a perfect balance with nature.

Will that person be you?

The Subtle Change from
Principles to Rules

Prologue

PROLOGUE: THE SUBTLE CHANGE FROM PRINCIPLES TO RULES

CONTENTS

Introduction — 5

From Eden to Woodstock — 8

Meadow Improvement — 12

What Does it All Mean? — 15

INTRODUCTION

In the lazy summer days of 2007, the world appeared to be getting its groove back. Few, if any, were the signs pointing to the financial catastrophe that was about to unfold.

Yet despite the feeling of relative calm and optimism, it was clear that a deep and permanent change was occurring at the very base of society. Suspicion was beginning to replace trust and goodwill amongst men.

This prologue is a compilation of three essays that were written during the summer of 2007 and first published in October 2010. They deal with a revelation that was given to us as we were attending a breakfast presentation on upcoming changes to the US accounting standards. Instead of fighting off the drowsiness which usually accompanies listening to accounting jargon, we found ourselves grappling with a deeply disturbing truth that increasingly defines life in America to this day.

American society, which had built itself and

created an unprecedented dynamism by operating on the basis of tacitly agreed upon principles, was now turning to the blunt instrument of rules as the basis for relationships.

An understanding of this subtle shift in American thinking will greatly aid one in understanding the seemingly inexplicable changes that they see all around them.

Clearly, rules have always been a part of life. They are nothing new. What is new is the power that is now being ascribed to rules. In America, it was often the case that a rule would be written and modified on the basis of an underlying principle. Rules for the sake of having them did not make much sense.

Now, circa 2012, the power is continuing to shift to the rules themselves. While the hallmark of principles is that they are flexible enough to adapt to constantly changing circumstances, rules tend to serve as a kind of concrete for society that, as it hardens, completely paralyzes anything that finds itself trapped within it.

Societies based on rules are nothing new. In fact, they are sadly becoming the norm throughout the world. Perhaps the clearest high level distinction between a society that operates on the basis of principles and one that operates on a basis of rules is whether it finds its legal basis in English Common Law, which generally produces outcomes based on equity before the law and a reasonable standard; and Napoleonic Code, with its strict adherence to written rules which often have little flexibility regarding the individual circumstance that are being examined.

THE SUBTLE CHANGE FROM PRINCIPLES TO RULES

These essays deal with the shift, then, from America's predisposition to operate on the basis of English Common Law to that of the rigidity of Napoleonic Code, and the inevitable consequences of making this shift.

The eternal question that we present here, "deer" reader, is whether or not one will stay in the meadow once as this shift occurs.

FROM EDEN TO WOODSTOCK

We recently attended a brief seminar that was entitled "GAAP Update." This title, to anyone who is not an accountant, may sound like some sort of fashion show. While we had hoped to observe some of the latest models of pocket protectors, the only thing that any reasonable person could observe to be in fashion was a decreasing reliance on professional judgment and increasing scrutiny, oversight, and more rules in the accounting profession.

In order to properly understand the above observation, we must first attempt to understand what GAAP is. GAAP, while not addictive, should be taken in small doses. As such, we will proceed to administer it in as small of doses as possible so that we can avoid the common side effects of confusion, drowsiness, and its other less understood attacks upon the human psyche.

GAAP, for those of you who have been fortunate enough to avoid the acronym thus far, stands for

"Generally Accepted Accounting Principles." According to Wikipedia:

"GAAP is the standard framework of guidelines for financial accounting. It includes the standards, conventions, and rules accountants follow in recording and summarizing transactions, and in the preparation of financial statements."

Wikipedia goes on to list the principles by which GAAP is guided by as the principles of Sincerity, Permanence of Methods, Non-Compensation, Prudence, Continuity, and Periodicity.

The presenter at the seminar, a brilliant local CPA, alluded to what we are now calling the subtle change from principles to rules when he mentioned that the words *"should"* and *"must"* were now explicitly defined in the new accounting guidelines in such a way that it had all but eliminated professional judgment from his profession.

His statements referred to the new requirements that the Statement of Accounting Standards 102, entitled *"Defining Professional Requirements in Statements on Auditing Standards,"* enjoined upon those condemned to his chosen profession. Where the word *"must"* appears, the accountant is to understand that the requirement is unconditional and must be performed. This is straightforward enough, and even highly trained professionals would have trouble arguing this definition.

It is the stated definition of the word *"should,"* which has from time immortal been the fallback for the imprudent when explaining why something was not done, which took the man aback. For the word *"should,"* from now to eternity, shall indicate a *"presumptively mandatory requirement,"* which for practical purposes, makes it just another spelling of the word "*must*."

On the surface, this sounds like a simple and presumably necessary clarification made in the name of making the writings of accountants more accessible to the general public and the ethics of the general public more accessible to accountants.

The deeper truth, the one that our brilliant local CPA alluded to, is that trust in professional judgment has disintegrated and the need for specific, carefully worded instructions that remove the need for flawed professional judgment is taking its place. This should alarm us all, as the accounting profession is by no means the only field that this subtle change is taking place in.

*{**Editor's note**: If you would like to witness for yourself the alarming rate of the expansion of rules written by agencies of the Federal Government, a peek at regulations.gov at any given time will give you a general idea of the startling proliferation of rules in society.}*

Any institution that is organized by human beings, such as a company, a religion, a government, or a football team, follows a pattern. Observe closely, *deer (sic)* reader, and see if you can pull an example from your own experience. These institutions begin with some sort of principle or set of principles. The person or persons, whom we will call the founders of the institution, understand the principles upon which they were founded and tacitly operate according to these principles.

When something is in its genesis, it is fresh and exciting. Possibilities bound about, like deer in a meadow in early spring. It is a thing to behold.

THE SUBTLE CHANGE FROM PRINCIPLES TO RULES

People flock to this bounding, this life, to simply breathe it in and to somehow be a part of it.

"Let it always be this way!" they say, *"I love this! How can I join?"*

The founders may or may not have decided how one can join. In the beginning, at the genesis of the institution, it hardly matters. If people are not allowed to join formally, they will do so by imitation. Such is the charismatic nature of an attractive institution that is run on sound principles.

At this stage, whether formally invited or not, people flock to the institution in great multitudes. Everyone wants to bound with the deer, drink from the stream, to lie in the grass.

Then, something begins to happen. The people, who were not there at the genesis, do not understand why the deer are bounding. And when the deer try to explain this to them, the people may not understand or perhaps may disagree with the reasons given for their joyful bounding. In this miscommunication, the principles get lost or distorted.

Nevertheless, the people agree that the bounding must continue, and increase, by all means. They continue to flock to the meadow. Soon, because of the crowds, the bounding area becomes a mosh pit, the water in the stream becomes undrinkable, and the grass turns to mud.

In the blink of an eye, the once fair meadow full of bounding deer has quickly turned into a scene from Woodstock.

MEADOW IMPROVEMENT

The once vibrant meadow and its subsequent demise provide us with a handy metaphor from which to gain an understanding of the difference between principles and rules and what it means as we navigate together this subtle yet incredibly important cultural change in society.

We pick up the scene at our meadow in the aftermath of Woodstock. It has become obvious to everyone in the meadow, both deer and persons alike, that the meadow is no longer the utopia that they had entered. The people become desperate to understand what went wrong and more importantly how to keep it from going wrong again in the future.

How will they go about this? First, they cordon off a bounding area, so that bounding may continue, albeit in a limited fashion. Other areas are then cordoned off and efforts are made to revive the grass in these areas. It is prohibited to enter into these areas until it has been deemed "suitable for bounding." Next, they decide to construct a canal

THE SUBTLE CHANGE FROM PRINCIPLES TO RULES

system in part of the meadow and allow the stream to "revive" itself within its newfound confinements. Water from the stream and canals is then rationed, which, in turn, limits bounding. This limitation on bounding, as envisioned, seems to rejuvenate the meadow for a time.

At this stage, something peculiar; a paradox, if you will, begins to take place. The people in the meadow begin to see that, although bounding now has become a limited an increasingly coveted activity, their other projects seem to have achieved their aims, the grass is growing and the stream is beginning to clear up. Heartened by their success, they begin to dedicate more time and energy to meadow improvement and less time to the act of bounding.

There is now scarcely time or space for bounding anyhow, and meadow improvement is a much more worthy cause. Why just look! We have grass growing where no one can bound and our canal system now provides more rations of water for more people who are not bounding. What could be better?

The clear answer, though few people now recall it, is the very reason that people began to flock to the meadow in the first place: The freedom of bounding in a meadow! Joyful, unadulterated bounding without water rations and cordoned off grassy areas.

Now, however, nobody dares to say these things out loud, because everyone knows that meadow improvement has become vital, and that bounding, while entertaining, must be done on an extremely limited and controlled basis, with a careful eye on the grass and the stream, lest the area be disturbed again and they find it in need of further improvement.

Of course the original deer, their bounding, and their founding principles are now long gone, searching for another meadow in which to freely bound about. Some who remain in the meadow are still searching for these principles and long for the days when all will bound freely again.

However, since most of those who remain were either unaware of or are in some stage of disagreement with the original principles, the "why" of the boundless joy that they once beheld; meadow improvement continues and the deer and their principles are idolized but rarely sought after and never emulated.

Why is this so? The clear answer, of course, is that a return to those principles would lead to too much bounding, and everyone knows that too much bounding leads to ruined meadows.

So what is the point of this tale, deer *(sic)* reader? What can we learn from a humble accounting lecture, bounding deer, and meadow improvement projects? In other words, what does it all mean???

WHAT DOES IT ALL MEAN?

At this point, we are forced to step back from the mud, ponder the events unfolding in the meadow, and ask the questions that are raised in the parable, for they are of the utmost importance.

The parable highlights the subtle yet important difference between principles and rules. In the meadow parable, the activities and projects referred to as meadow improvement represent rules. Rules are made by those who either do not fully understand or do not desire to adhere to the principles of an activity and are generally imposed with the stated purpose of maintaining or improving the status quo.

Once a human institution, as the meadow was to represent, makes the subtle change from being guided by principles to being governed by rules, these rules fill the meadow with cordoned off areas and canals until no one can freely move about within them.

A glance at the following definitions will help us to better understand the conceptual difference between principles and rules. A principle, according to the Encyclopedia; *"signifies a point (or points) of probability on a subject (i.e. the principle of creativity), which allows for the formation of rule or norm or law by (human) interpration of the phenomena (events) that can be created."* By contrast, a rule, according to dictionary.com, is; *"a principle or regulation governing conduct, action, procedure, arrangement, etc."* Making a clear distinction between principles and rules is confusing because the terms are often used interchangeably to define two concepts that could not be more different. This is why the change from principles to rules may be said to be subtle.

Given that the distinction appears to be subtle, we must attempt to compare and contrast these concepts in the following terms: Principles make things possible. Principles create. Rules govern conduct or regulate. Rules destroy. With this understanding, we can now postulate that, while principles tend to create rules, rules tend to destroy principles once the propagation of rules dwarfs the principles that created them. It is as if an invisible prison is constructed by the growing threat of going to a real one.

Does this mean that principles are bad because they create rules? By no means, in the same way, rules are not bad either, but principles must be held above the rules that they create in order for the principles to maintain their power to create and make things possible. Once rules are allowed to dominate, they thrust aside principles and a prison begins to quickly construct itself.

This is what our brilliant local CPA was alluding to in the GAAP Update seminar when he mentioned that the word "*should*" in of some of the pronouncements had been changed to "*must*." For this careful choice of words is perhaps the clearest manifestation of this subtle shift in American society, circa 2012.

The word "*should*" bestows some glimmer of freedom of choice upon the hearer. As in "*You should wear a jacket, its cold.*" While the word should implies a strong suggestion that one would do well to heed, it is understood that one is free to ignore it, albeit at their peril. Once the word "*must*" is placed in the same sentence, this freedom is removed and the only thing that remains is the expectation of punishment for non-compliance.

This type of subtle but intentional choice of words can only lead to resentment and violence in the meadow, where those guilty of stealing water rations for their parched fellow meadow dwellers and for crossing into a cordoned off area are either incarcerated, banished, or exterminated in an increasingly futile attempt by the meadow improvers to keep the meadow clean. While those dwelling in the meadow may gradually adjust to this dire state of affairs, it will be clear to all external observers that the once vibrant meadow has turned into a gruesome cross between a pig sty and a slaughter house.

Such is the fate of a society in which rules are employed to remove all semblance of freedom of its inhabitants. It is not a question of if, but when, and it is abundantly clear that the principles of liberty and self-determination are the only antidote to the poison of rules once they have overwhelmed the principles that gave rise to them.

And what of the deer who began all of the bounding in the meadow in the first place? Wouldn't they have stayed around to ensure the freedom of bounding? It is perhaps the greatest of ironies that these deer, who so fervently loved bounding and whose activities attracted the very people who would stifle and destroy it, would simply bound to another meadow as the first restrictions on bounding were being drafted.

For it is the very nature of true freedom to respect the right to freedom of others, even if others use that right to destroy the very freedom that has been accorded to them.

What is Truth?

On the Nature of Empire

Volume I

WHAT IS TRUTH?
ON THE NATURE OF EMPIRE

VOLUME I

CONTENTS

Empire: An Introduction	21
Fiat Currency: The Poisonous Money Supply	27
Turf: Maintaining the Peace	29
Debt: A Corrosive Symptom of Empire	31
Empire Ensures the Promotion of the Morally Corrupt	36
Jon Corzine: An Example of Leadership in The Modern Day Imperial System	42
The Better Way	47
Required Reading for All Human Beings	53
What is Truth?	57
Conclusion	64
Appendix A: The Catechism of Non-Resistance	68

EMPIRE: AN INTRODUCTION

empire -/'empī(ə)r/- noun -1. An extensive group of states or countries under a single supreme authority or oligarchy.

Derived from the Latin imperium, the word Empire has come to embody the concept of dominance on a grand scale. From the time of the original Akkadian, Mayan, and Egyptian Empires to the more recent Greek, Roman, and British versions, the ignoble goal of all Imperial activities has been to establish and maintain primacy in the affairs of men and women throughout the known world.

Proof of this is found in the behavior of the heads of Empire, known as emperors and empresses, who invariably come to embody the ultimate conceit of the imperial mindset by attempting to establish themselves as a deity. The conceit is always fatal, for this ridiculous presumption has the nasty side-affect of destroying any shred of legitimacy that the head of Empire may have previously established with those subject to them. However, whether or not the emperor publically manifests a claim to deity by demanding reverence reserved for the truly divine, those who have reigned in the emperor's chair have invariably come to assume that they had, at their disposal, the divine right to liquidate any and all threats to their claim to ultimate power over their fellow mortals.

In the twenty first century, it has become clear to most that there is no divine right or imperative for the existence of an Empire on the earth. As such, an ever-increasing number of peoples have thrown off the yoke of Empire in favor of what has become known as a democratic model of collective governance.

Yet simply changing the rules of governance has not put an end to the core ideals of Empire. This is evident in the fact that the hallmarks of Imperial rule, namely the tendencies toward a central monopoly on the use of force and the right to demand tribute, have been largely retained by governments today that are elected democratically. How can this be?

The concept of Empire is a construction of men, and is largely the result of a tolerance by the many of what is essentially antisocial behavior by a few. As stated above, an Empire, at its base, consists of a monopoly on the use of force that evolves into a monopoly on the right to demand tribute.

Living under Imperial rule is not man's natural state, and it will eventually come into conflict with mankind's natural disposition for autonomy, commonly known as freedom or the right to self-determination.

Why, then, do the many tolerate the antisocial behavior by a few that ultimately leads to Imperial rule? The answer is that Empires do not appear overnight. They emerge over relatively long time horizons. As such, those who become subject to another's Imperial ambition have often made a subconscious choice to tolerate the antisocial behavior as the perceived cost of fighting it individually far outweighs the incremental loss of freedom that they suffer. Indeed, until an Empire approaches its blow off phase, it may even appear to its subjects to provide many social benefits. However, these benefits always come at a great human cost, a cost that is almost always obscured from those who receive them. In the end, the price is paid by all, as the Empire turns on even those who receive the benefits in a desperate attempt to hold onto its position.

It should come as no surprise, then, that there is no historical evidence of an Empire spontaneously arising by mutual consent. On the contrary, Empires are created and expanded by subjugating a territory and the peoples that inhabit it via either the threat or actual use of military force. Once subjugated, the Empire attempts to consolidate its control of the territory by exacting tribute from its subjects. From ancient times up to today, an Empire's demand for tribute ultimately manifests itself in taking control of the food supply.

One of the more poignant historical examples of this can be found in the Biblical book of Genesis, where Joseph advises the emperor of Egypt at the time, Pharaoh, to store up the Egyptian grain production for a time in anticipation of a seven-year famine. Pharaoh subsequently sold the grain back to the Egyptians and foreigners during the famine. While the story generally has a happy ending, it is a stark example of the Imperial prerogative to confiscate property via taxation.

Given this example, it is no surprise that the first known system of taxation existed in Ancient Egypt around 3000 BCE - 2800 BCE.

Paradoxically, the subjects of Empire, who could just as easily eat from the foodstuffs they produce as well as store up their own rainy day funds, find themselves rendering their harvests to the representatives of the Empire, in the case of the Pharaoh, a full 20% of their production, only to be forced to beg them back at a future date when the need for them inevitably arises.

The Paradox is furthered in that the Empire, in attempting to maintain primacy via various forms of taxation, ultimately ensures its demise, as the inherent waste in the Imperial model overwhelms its ability to extract further tribute from its subjects. The mechanism of taxation itself causes the Empire to weaken, as it indirectly encourages sub optimum activity and in the worst case, inactivity and waste by those who are in a position to receive the benefits derived from the tax proceeds.

Long before the Empire becomes aware of its weakened state, the subjects themselves are often the first to realize that the Emperor is wearing no clothes, to borrow Mr. Andersen's metaphor. Those with the means and the initiative will move to escape the withering grasp of the failing Empire. Those who do not leave are often left to perish in a futile effort to either defend the Empire or oppose it through the same force of arms by which the Empire first came to their lands. For an Empire must ultimately demand allegiance from its subjects, and its intolerance for dissention will tend to increase in direct proportion to the level of weakness of the Empire.

As such, for an Empire to perpetuate itself, it must rely entirely on the force of arms when necessary and coercive propaganda at all times in an ultimately futile attempt to assure it retains the primitive right to meddle in the affairs of others. In the final blow off phase, which is marked by civil wars and emigration, such as the one currently playing out in Syria, the Empire will resort almost exclusively to the use of arms to squash dissention.

Yet the maintenance of Empire, like the air travel industry, is in every case a losing proposition. It is an utter and complete waste of time and money. To maintain an Empire requires an ever-increasing amount of human and intellectual capital that are depleted in ever increasing quantities as the Empire slides into history's dustbin, where it will simply attach itself to the long list of Empires that were.

The concept of Empire has always been lethal to human existence and prosperity. However, for some reason it is romanticized in the human psyche. The purpose of this volume is to gain an understanding of the true nature of Empire and, to convince the reader that Empire, and by extension large scale government, is not only unnecessary, but a great hindrance to human progress. This volume also explores why the Imperial model virtually ensures that the worst elements of humanity will rise to power, where they will ultimately impose their will on their fellow humans by violence. For the violent outcomes that Empires invariably produce are not exceptions to the rule, nor are they merely the norm.

They are literally guaranteed by design.

Once we have grasped the true nature of Empire, we will then will explore the only known antidote to Empire and explore the only possible means for mankind to rid itself of the lethal effects of Empire on the earth.

Finally, we address Pontius Pilate's infamous inquiry, to Jesus of Nazareth before His public trial:

"What is truth?"

It is a question that has been left to humanity for two millennia, and it is time that it be answered, for in the answer lies our common fate.

FIAT CURRENCY: THE POISONOUS MONEY SUPPLY

In order to understand the nature of Empire, we must begin by briefly examining how the Imperial mechanism works to corrode the basis of society; its economic activity that expresses itself through trade. For any Empire to be effective, it must gain at a minimum the illusion of control over the economic activity of its subjects. In order to gain control of the economy, the Empire must first commandeer the money supply. This action is necessarily followed by a program of creating currency via fiat, or Imperial decree. The money that it creates by fiat then becomes a lethal poison to the productive sectors of society.

Fiat money may look and act like money created through economic activity, but it has an entirely different chemical makeup, and injecting it into the economy in ever increasing doses will eventually lead to the very death of the economy, the cause of which is a currency overdose which ultimately rewards sloth and makes the planning and execution of any productive activity futile.

The world that we live in functions on immutable natural laws, laws that are not imposed by men, but by nature itself. One of the most basic natural laws is the law of supply and demand, which is today associated with the discipline of economics. This law, which states that as the supply of a good or service increases or decreases relative to the demand for such good or service, the market price for the good or service will tend adjust accordingly, and will usually have an inverse relationship to the increase or decrease in supply.

The law of supply and demand is the basis for the market mechanism of price formation. Price signals set by the market via this mechanism, in turn, are the basis for nearly every human activity. On this earth, men and women will prosper as far as measurable material wealth is concerned to the extent that they are free to respond to the demands of this natural law. It follows, then, that men and women are best able to respond to the demands of this natural law when they live under conditions of relative peace.

TURF: MAINTAINING THE PEACE

The maintenance of the peace is the ultimate value proposition of the Empire. However, the existence of an Empire rarely leads to peace. In fact, once an Empire is established, it will tend to undertake an inordinate amount of violence in order to maintain the peace. Like the mafia boss who extracts payments for "protection" from the business owners on his turf, the Empire comes to demand tribute under essentially the same premise.

While the irony that the mafia boss is extracting protection payments in exchange for not robbing the business owner via an unexpected act of aggression initiated by the mafia boss himself is lost on few, most people fail to understand that this is the same *modus operandi* that the Empire employs when exacting tribute from its subjects.

As any mafia boss can attest, the "*maintenance of the peace*" business model is ultimately a losing proposition. Its Achilles heel is that it relies on the threat of superior force to be effective. As the mafia boss accumulates the means to exert superior force over those on his turf and exacts an ever-increasing amount of tribute in order to maintain this advantage, he will quickly find that his turf is being vacated and avoided at an alarming rate. Those who don't need to stick around will leave, and there will be few, if any, who will see the controlled turf as an attractive place to live.

The economic imbalances that this scenario brings about will lead the entire turf economy to run a net deficit. The only way it can keep running is by borrowing.

DEBT: A CORROSIVE SYMPTOM OF EMPIRE

The Empire has the problem of the mafia boss on a much larger scale. While more complex, it essentially operates on the same loss generating *"maintenance of the peace"* business model. It is a business model that enjoys inverse economies of scale. The larger it becomes, the more deeply in debt it must go to maintain its advantage.

In this way, it can be said that debt is a symptom of Empire. At first, the Empire can pretend to have the ability to exact tribute in quantities sufficient to maintain its operations. However, over time the extraction of tribute, which is usually done in an unpredictable and non-uniform fashion, will cause irreparable disruptions in the underlying economy. This harm is multiplied by the obligation to render tribute in the Empire's fiat currency, which forces the subjects to take the poison and deal in the Empire's corrupted currency units.

The underlying economy of the Empire consists

of men and women trying to comply with the daily demands of the natural law of supply and demand. If these efforts are sufficiently disrupted, they will overwhelm the subject's ability to support themselves and pay what has become known as their "fair share" for the "right" to be protected by the Empire.

Human progress is a fickle thing that, contrary to what one may have experienced in their lifetime, is not a given. Most of the 19th and 20th centuries have been marked by the general acceleration of human progress. Unfortunately, a good deal of this progress over the past one hundred years has been realized by the accumulation of a completely unnatural amount of debt alongside the creation of a completely unnatural increase in the amount of fiat currency in world.

On one hand, the accumulation of debt and the creation of fiat currency have enabled men to make technological advances that were not even dreamed of a generation before. On the other, this debt and currency have created severe imbalances in the natural world for which the only cure is the liquidation of said debt and fiat currency which will lead to an uncomfortable change in the daily activities for many.

Debt that occurs normally in an economy, that is, debt incurred by businesses that have business models which will allow them to realistically pay it back through real economic earnings will, when left to its own devices, achieve equilibrium. In the productive economy, credit is created in response to anticipated increases in the capital stock.

However, with the advent of Empire, debt

issuance is increasingly associated not with increases in the supply of capital or productive capacity in an economy, but by simple decree of the imperial authority. The creation of debt by Imperial decree begins when the Empire is no longer able to extract tribute from its subjects in sufficient quantities to fund its excesses and is almost always the predecessor of a dramatic increase in the amount of fiat currency created by the Empire. While few will acknowledge the fact until a much later date, an Empire generally begins to accumulate debt as it begins to decline in power. In fact, the inability to operate without incurring additional debt is the hallmark of an Empire on its way into history's dustbin.

The Empires throughout history that have survived any amount of time have found it necessary to expand their operations beyond the simpleton "maintenance of the peace" business model of the mafia boss. These Empires inevitably expand their operations to include any number of business lines that operate under another business model that is guaranteed to result in heavy losses: The redistribution of wealth.

This is where the Empire begins to accelerate its already ensured demise. With its nascent consolidation of the power to resort to violence, the Empire inevitably expands its operations to interfere with activities far beyond the maintenance of a common defense. Most of these extensions of power are more difficult to palate for those subject to the Empire. Naturally, the subjects who are asked to fund a greater portion of the Empire's activities, those who are considered wealthy, begin to look for ways to lower their tribute. As these are generally the more cunning of the citizens, they will be ultimately successful in achieving this goal.

The lower tribute that the Empire experiences invariably coincides with increasing monetary outlays by the Empire, which it must, as we have explored above, fund by issuing debt. Yet debt issued by an Empire has nothing to do with an anticipated increase in the capital stock, rather, the proceeds are used to fund deficits as the tandem "maintenance of the peace/wealth redistribution" business models go to work destroying the remaining capital stock of both the Empire and those who are subject to it.

As the capital stock begins to dwindle, the Empire naturally progresses to using its monopoly on force to take direct control of the food supply and other industries that are deemed essential. What is and is not considered essential is naturally left up to the Empire's sole discretion. Those subject to the Empire are required to render crops as tribute and then to accept a ration of food from the Empire. Today, this process takes place indirectly via the dual use of fiat currency and the tax code or welfare systems established by the Empire. While the mechanism is obscured, the outcome is the same.

Once the Empire has control of the food supply, the supply "mysteriously" begins to dwindle. The fate of the products of the other industries that the Empire had deemed essential is the same, and the ruin of society is then complete. When scarcity overtakes the subjects who remain beholden to the Empire, they tend to become restless.

At this point, whatever ideological pretense the

Empire was founded on is sacrificed in the blind pursuit of a de facto communism. The end game, which has played out numerous times throughout history, involves starvation, moral deprivation, violence, and revolution.

As the script has played out over the centuries, civil persons everywhere have been known to murmur, "There must be a better way." A better way there is, indeed, but we must first deal with Empire's most disturbing attribute: The ensured promotion of those persons who possess the worst of moral compasses into the ranks of leadership.

EMPIRE ENSURES THE PROMOTION OF THE MORALLY CORRUPT

It seems that such poor management, as described in the previous chapter, must have its origins somewhere. It also would seem logical that, given that so many Empires have risen and fallen, causing such widespread suffering, that today's world leaders are operating with the benefit of these past experiences and have either mastered or abandoned the dual mandate of *"maintenance of the peace/wealth redistribution,"* when it comes to large scale governance.

Alas, this is not the case, for Empire, whose origin lies in one group's ability to exert physical violence upon another, is a system that guarantees that those who lead will be the ones who are the most devoid of compassion and morality and, consequently, will be the absolute worst managers possible.

How can this be? Why is it that those that possess the most dysfunctional moral compass seem to come out on top? For insight, we look to a prophecy first uttered by the Biblical prophet,

WHAT IS TRUTH? ON THE NATURE OF EMPIRE

Isaiah, in relation to Empire:

"And I will make boys their princes, and infants shall rule over them. And the people will oppress one another, every one his fellow and every one his neighbor; the youth will be insolent to the elder, and the despised to the honorable,"

Isaiah 3:4-5

Unlike racketeering and the accumulation of debt, which may be experienced and fully understood by only a small portion of the subjects of the Empire, this most disturbing facet of the nature of Empire is one that most can directly relate to. The tendency for the unscrupulous elements of society to rise to positions of leadership in an Imperial system can be illustrated by truthfully undertaking to answer the following set of questions:

Have you ever complained about a politician? The government? How about your boss? The current state of society? If you haven't, you are indeed a rarity in this day in age, for one need only pick up a newspaper or listen to a radio station to understand that there is much complaining, and seemingly much to complain about in the world today.

How did we arrive at this state of affairs? If democracy is supposed to deliver the cream of the crop in terms of leadership in the government, why does it seem that most politicians are the epitome of immoral liars? The answer is that democracy, like all other forms of rule that rely upon a monopoly of the use of force, is in no way superior to the previous forms of Imperial rule and large-scale government that it has come to replace.

It is a bitter irony that when the votes are tallied and the people have spoken, it is inevitable that those who lack morals, scruples, and have a penchant for sociopathic behavior, are most likely to grasp, nay, have the scepter of power thrust upon them by the Empire.

Friedrich Hayek, or F.A. Hayek, an economist born in Austria-Hungary in 1899, who witnessed the atrocities undertaken in the name of Empire during World War I, developed a theory on this very subject. Hayek presented his theory in a section of what is now known as his war cry against central planning, the "Road to Serfdom."

In a section of the book entitled *"Why the Worst Get to the Top,"* Hayek writes:

"There are strong reasons for believing that the worst features of the totalitarian systems are phenomena which totalitarianism is certain sooner or later to produce.

Just as the democratic statesman who sets out to plan economic life will soon be confronted with the alternative of either assuming dictatorial powers or abandoning his plans, so the totalitarian leader would soon have to choose between disregard of ordinary morals and failure. It is for this reason that the unscrupulous are likely to be more successful in a society tending toward totalitarianism. Who does not see this has not yet grasped the full width of the gulf which separates totalitarianism from the essentially individualist Western civilization."

As man has generally chosen to pursue the Totalitarian, or what we call the Imperial model, it follows that those thrust into power would be among the most immoral, unscrupulous, human beings on the planet.

In summary, the Imperial model, and the increasingly totalitarian leanings of large-scale democratic government, unwittingly promote the worst individuals to positions of power, as they are best suited to carry out the immoral and contradictory demands that are invariably made of the persons occupying positions of power in such a system.

Depressed? Don't be. It doesn't have to be this way.

The acts which are required to carry out an economic system doomed to failure, which the Imperial model guarantees, ensures that those who are promoted to leadership in the economic sphere of Empire would also be the worst amongst society in terms of adhering to any sort of moral code. They will be individuals who have chosen to pursue the economic or political program above the obligations of morality, no matter what the cost. They possess the rare ability to mute their conscience and oversee acts that are increasingly despicable and outrageous in pursuit of the blunt aims of the program.

They are all too familiar with the term, "collateral damage," for they are the ones who have coined it.

Hayek goes on to argue that as the Totalitarian (read Imperial) economic and social program inevitably begins to fail, the leader of said system would increasingly deem it necessary to employ a larger number of individuals to enforce the increasing sacrifices required to continue the program. He offers three reasons why this inevitable outcome further assures that the leader surrounds himself with and encourages the promotion of those who are capable of the worst forms of moral corruption:

"First, the higher the education and intelligence of individuals become, the more their tastes and views are differentiated. If we wish to find a high degree of uniformity in outlook, we have to descend to the regions of your moral and intellectual standards where the more primitive instincts prevail. This does not mean that the majority of people have low moral standards; it merely means that the largest group of people whose values are very similar are the people with low standards.

Second, since this group is not large enough to give sufficient weight to the leader's endeavors, he will have to increase their numbers by converting more to the same simple creed. He must gain the support of the docile and gullible, who have no strong convictions of their own but are ready to accept a ready-made system of values if it is only drummed into their ears sufficiently loudly and frequently. It will be those whose vague and imperfectly formed ideas are easily swayed and whose passions and emotions are readily aroused who will thus swell the ranks of the totalitarian party.

Third, to weld together a closely coherent body of supporters, the leader must appeal to a common human weakness. It seems to be easier for people to agree on a negative program — on the hatred of an enemy, on the envy of those better off – than on any positive task. The contrast between the "we" and the "they" is consequently always employed by those who seek the allegiance of huge masses. The enemy may be internal, like the "Jew" in Germany or the "kulak" in Russia, or he may be external. In any case, this technique has the great advantage of leaving the leader greater freedom of action than would almost any positive program.

Advancement within a totalitarian group or party depends largely on a willingness to do immoral things."

The Imperial model, then, far from being a viable alternative form of government that can be espoused as mankind continues its inevitable march towards progressively higher living standards, instead assures a slow march towards a society that openly ignores the rule of law and, as a consequence, quickly becomes devoid of morality.

The ideological battle between True Capitalism, which we will deal with in Volume V, and the Imperial model of governance, is much more than a simple choice of economic systems, rather, it is a reflection of the moral code upon which a majority of the society's members will come to base their actions.

JON CORZINE: AN EXAMPLE OF LEADERSHIP IN THE MODERN DAY IMPERIAL SYSTEM

We will now state plainly something we have alluded to in this volume: The nature of Empire is alive and well in the democratically elected governments of today's nation states.

As such, all of the hallmarks of the Imperial system, from the monopoly on the use of force, to the extraction of tribute, down through the phenomenon of men and women of the worst moral fiber increasingly advancing into leadership positions as the once quaint idea of government for the people by the people falls victim to the temptations and illusion of imagined Imperial omnipotence.

The United States of America has recently produced many shining examples of the phenomenon of the worst rising to the top. However, the case of Jon Corzine, former governor of New Jersey and former CEO of the now infamous investment bank, MF Global, embodies all that is wrong with the modern day Imperial structure, which is a grotesque melding of democratic rule and what is commonly known as crony capitalism, where enterprises which were birthed in true capitalism are now dependent upon favors granted by the government for their survival. A survival that is granted and ensured because the enterprises provide something that the government relies upon to further exert its dual monopolies on the use of force and the collection of tribute.

Senator John Corzine

Mr. Corzine is a career investment banker and politician. In other words, he has been firmly indoctrinated and skillfully trained in two of the most destructive trades known to mankind.

Mr. Corzine's case is best illustrated by the fact

that he allegedly saw nothing wrong with raiding the cash accounts of MF Global's clients in a vain attempt to stave off the firm's imminent bankruptcy, which was eventually filed on October 31, 2011. There is no way to sugar coat what happened in the days leading up to MF Global's demise. MF Global allegedly robbed its clients' accounts to meet its own obligations. Mr. Corzine's actions in this case were nearly indistinguishable from those of politicians when it comes to economic matters. For in the operations of the government's treasury, it has become a common and acceptable practice to rob a legally established trust fund and replace the funds with the government's IOUs.

Mr. Corzine is but the most recent example of the level of hubris and moral corruption required to occupy a high level post in the government and financial sectors circa 2011.

The MF Global bankruptcy and subsequent actions taken by the regulators have called into question whether or not the rule of law will prove supreme in such a situation. As a society increasingly leans towards an Imperial model of authority, the excuses for ignoring the rule of law tend to proliferate. Again, we turn to the work of F.A. Hayek, who observed the inextricable link between the rule of law and Freedom when he wrote the following:

"NOTHING distinguishes more clearly a free country from a country under arbitrary government than the observance in the former of the great principles known as the Rule of Law. Stripped of technicalities, this means that government in all its

actions is bound by rules fixed and announced beforehand."

Modern day excuses for ignoring the rule of law often come in the form of appealing to a greater good such as, *"These actions are taken in order to protect the American people,"* and *"These actions have been taken to ensure the stability of the Financial System,"* to cite two oft repeated examples.

However, with each unilateral trampling that a previously enjoyed liberty suffers at the hands of Empire, the subjects begin to ask themselves with increasing regularity, *"are we safer?"* or, *"Is the financial system is more stable?"*

These are important questions, for the collective answer to these questions will reveal whether or not the government is serving the people or if it has begun to slide down the slippery slope of Imperial rule, for despite claims to the contrary, there is no way to strike a perfect balance between freedom and governance. A government is constantly tending either one way or the other, towards freedom or Empire. There is no ideological middle ground.

The governments of the world that tend towards Empire are tirelessly advancing a failed program. It should come as no surprise, then, that nearly every action that the governments take seem to have made the original problem worse. To further confuse the matter, any gains made by the people despite the tinkering of the Imperial apparatus are held up by the Empire as proof of the wisdom of the Empire's program.

It is clear that as long as institutions and governments embrace the Imperial ideology, those who are best able to ignore basic morality and the rule of law are most likely to populate their halls of power. It should come as no surprise, then, that man's only hope for peace and justice is to reject the Imperial model entirely and to embrace Freedom. Only then will lasting peace and prosperity be attainable.

In what at first appears to be a further paradox, the Imperial apparatus cannot be thrust away by the force of arms, for in choosing this route, the force that opposes the current Empire becomes simply its successor in the doomed dance of history. To truly reject an Empire and change the course of history once again towards human progress, one must choose the Better Way.

THE BETTER WAY

In previous chapters, we have explored the nature of Empire and found that it is necessarily founded and maintained by a monopoly on the use of force. This monopoly has, as its logical end, the effect of destroying the capital stock of a society. This is accomplished by demands for tribute, or taxation, which amounts to the confiscation of individual wealth. The confiscated wealth is then consumed by the Empire via warfare, whose destructive nature need not be further explored, and welfare, which by nature rewards sloth and penalizes productivity.

*{**Editor's Note**: Here we must make the clear distinction between charity, which is a voluntary action taken by a willing individuals to help their fellow human beings and welfare, which is a system of Imperially mandated aid which ends in enslavement both for the recipient and provider.}*

When confronted with the fatal defect of Empire, the inevitable destruction of the capital stock of a society, the Imperial apologist offers support of the

Empire as either the lesser of two evils, implying that the ideological alternative, namely: Anarchy, would lead to chaos and an even greater destruction of life and capital, or may offer support for the existence of Empire in any number of religious texts and conclude that submission to government is God's will.

"I am an atheist with regards to government, for I have chosen to live in the Kingdom of God"

This refrain, which is all at once a rejection of human attempts at governance and the recognition of a divine imperative inherent in the human experience, takes the idea of Anarchy a step beyond an imagined void of governance as we present the Better Way. It is the method of change that civil persons over the centuries have searched for and, in their better moments, embraced.

The term Anarchy, perhaps not surprisingly, is generally associated with chaos and disorder. However, the state of anarchy, when properly understood apart from the negative connotations that have been thrust upon it, is nothing more than choosing to embrace what is the polar opposite of Empire.

Joel Bowman, managing editor over at the Daily Reckoning, explored this idea in a post entitled: *We're all Anarchists Now"*. In the post, Mr. Bowman deftly points out that anarchy is a concept that has been hijacked. In the same way that the term Liberalism has come to be associated with social progressives, anarchy has come to be associated with rebellious hoodlums. However, when properly understood, anarchy is the perfect antidote for the problem of Empire. As Mr. Bowman explains it:

"Properly understood, the term anarchy, which derives from the Greek anarchia, literally translates as, "without" + arkhos, "ruler." Freedom from being owned...enslaved...forced against one's will. Freedom to act voluntarily. Freedom to associate with whomever one so desires and under whatever conditions he or she sees fit...provided they do not diminish the ability of another to enjoy the same freedom."

In other words, anarchy declares that, all at once, there are no sovereigns and that every individual is sovereign. You can understand why this may upset Imperial apologists who cannot begin to imagine this worldview.

As for those who would support the *"necessary evils"* of perpetuating the Empire on religious grounds, we offer the following: Were the Empire to truly be God's agent on earth, it would cease to exist on logical grounds.

The logic is the following: From the beginning, God has desired direct communion with mankind. It is from a state of perfect communion with God that mankind has fallen, and it is to this state of perfect communion that mankind will return. How can this perfect communion exist if God requires an earthly, imperial authority to act on His behalf?

Yet the ultimate solution of Anarchy, where there is no sovereign, save God himself, or where every individual is a sovereign subject to God, depending upon one's preferred theology, would be the embodiment of a perfect communion between God and mankind. In fact, it is the only way that this type of relationship would be possible.

The problem, then, is not the existence of Empire; the Empire is simply the manifestation of man's failed belief system that *"Might makes right."* It is this failed belief system that must be vanquished.

Sadly, to study most of human history is to study the violent and destructive embodiment of the Might makes right mentality as Empires rise and fall, either to enemies from without or to revolutions from within. With every violent upheaval, most recently observed in what is now referred to as the Arab Spring, it becomes clear that the populace has simply exchanged one oppressive regime for another.

In fact, as one examines history, it becomes clear that the only large-scale social changes that have come about under the rule of Empire have come through the use of a tactic known as peaceful resistance. Who amongst us are not familiar with the name Mohandas Gandhi or Martin Luther King, Jr.? These men found that the key to large-scale social change lies in confronting injustices with peaceful resistance.

While Mohandas Gandhi and Martin Luther King, Jr. were able to bring about a great deal of liberation from within the Imperial apparatus under which the groups they came to represent were oppressed, their tactics, while admirable and effective, allowed them to achieve their aims only at the expense of a formal recognition of the Imperial apparatus. This outcome is debatable in the case of Gandhi, as his movement led to the eventual retreat of the British Imperial apparatus. However, present day India, as is the case with all world governments, continues to suffer from the problems that are inherent in the Imperial exercise of power by one group of persons over another, and it may be said that one yoke has been exchanged for another, albeit relatively lighter.

The key to permanent change, the type of change that will forever banish the tainted power of Empire from the earth, lies not in peaceful resistance, but in a tactic that is, in most cases, more widely practiced than acknowledged known as non-resistance. While peaceful resistance seeks to openly confront the Empire and effect change upon it while maintaining the basic structures of the Imperial apparatus, non-resistance neither violently opposes the Empire, nor does it endorse, either tacitly or expressly, any acts of aggression taken on behalf of the Empire. Non-resistance is a full and complete embrace of the concept that is best expressed in the simple yet powerful phrase; *"live and let live."* Peaceful non-resistance, in its purest form, is to live one's life as if the Empire does not exist.

It is the way revealed to us by Jesus of Nazareth, who chose to suffer and die at the hands of Empire in order to break the disease of Might makes right in the hearts of everyone. To open the way for a perfect communion with God.

This is the Better Way. His action trumped every argument that could ever be made in favor of Empire, and opened the doors to God's Kingdom, the reign of a Holy God over a perfect anarchy where there is only one rule, which is emblazoned on every heart:

"Love your neighbor as you love yourself"

REQUIRED READING FOR ALL HUMAN BEINGS

Leo Tolstoy, in his Christian-Anarchist work "The Kingdom of God is Within You," pays homage to Adin Ballou, an American preacher who was a colleague of William Lloyd Garrison, the great American Abolitionist. Ballou devoted 50 years of his life advocating for the doctrine of non-resistance. The basis for their belief in the doctrine is found in Jesus of Nazareth's command given during the Sermon on the Mount,

"Resist not evil"

Such was Ballou's conviction to the cause of non-resistance that He drafted the Catechism of Non-Resistance for his followers. The final section of the Catechism, which Ballou entitled, "Non-resistance is Salvation; Resistance is Ruin," is especially moving, so much so that we consider it required reading for all human beings.

Adin Ballou, before 1891

Non-resistance is Salvation; Resistance is Ruin.

It is incomparably less dangerous to act justly than unjustly, to submit to injuries than to resist them with violence, less dangerous even in one's relations to the present life. If all men refused to resist evil by evil our world would be happy.

Q. But so long as only a few act thus, what will happen to them?

A. If only one man acted thus, and all the rest agreed to crucify him, would it not be nobler for him to die in the glory of non-resisting love, praying for his enemies, than to live to wear the crown of Caesar stained with the blood of the slain? However, one man, or a thousand men, firmly resolved not to oppose evil by evil are far more free from danger by violence than those who resort to violence, whether among civilized or savage neighbors. The robber, the murderer, and the cheat will leave them in peace, sooner than those who oppose them with arms, and those who take up the sword shall perish by the sword, but those who seek after peace, and behave kindly and harmlessly, forgiving and forgetting injuries, for the most part enjoy peace, or, if they die, they die blessed. In this way, if all kept the ordinance of non-resistance, there would obviously be no evil nor crime. If the majority acted thus they would establish the rule of love and good will even over evil doers, never opposing evil with evil, and never resorting to force. If there were a moderately large minority of such men, they would exercise such a salutary moral influence on society that every cruel punishment would be abolished, and violence and feud would be replaced by peace and love. Even if there were only a small minority of them, they would rarely experience anything worse than the world's contempt, and meantime the world, though unconscious of it, and not grateful for it, would be continually becoming wiser and better for their unseen action on it. And if in the worst case some members of the minority were persecuted to death, in dying for the truth they would have left behind them their doctrine, sanctified by the blood of their martyrdom. Peace, then, to all who seek peace, and may overruling love be the imperishable heritage of every soul who obeys willingly Christ's word, "Resist not evil."

ADIN BALLOU.

The catechism can be read in its entirety in Appendix A of this volume.

The ultimate triumph of the doctrine of non-resistance may never be seen in a tangible fashion, for it takes the form of conquering not on a battlefield, but quietly, calling one soul at a time to peace with his fellow man. Non-resistance triumphs not through deployment of superior force or tactics, but through its marked refusal to meet violence with violence. The injustice of the Might Makes Right doctrine of Empire is best exposed not on the battlefield, but in those harrowing displays which take place when those who have claimed a monopoly on the use of force employ it against innocent victims, those who, in abandoning self preservation, claim the moral high ground for all to see.

When the Empire confronts non-resistance with force, it is the Empire that suffers the mortal blow, for the putrid truth of its nature is laid bare for all to see, and those persons with any shred of decency begin to distance themselves from it in earnest.

WHAT IS TRUTH?

The distinction between the ideological basis for all Empires is the failed Might makes right mentality, and what we have termed the Better Way, which can be summed up in the words of the Golden Rule: *"Love your neighbor as you love yourself,"* and the doctrine of non-resistance, was made clear to all in an event that can only be adequately described as the flashpoint in human history, the moment which literally opened the possibility for mankind to be able to choose the Better Way. It was the moment that truth was revealed to all of humanity.

This critical moment is related for us in the Gospel of John, chapter 18, verses 37 and 38:

37 "You are a king, then!" said Pilate. Jesus answered, "You say that I am a king. In fact, the reason I was born and came into the world is to testify to the truth. Everyone on the side of truth listens to me."

38 "What is truth?" retorted Pilate. With this he

went out again to the Jews gathered there and said, "I find no basis for a charge against him."

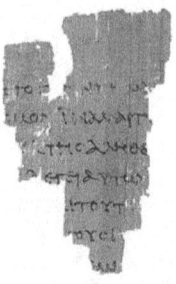

P52, an ancient papyrus inscribed with John 18:37-38

For those unfamiliar with the scene, which is expanded upon in John 38:28-40, this historic exchange between Jesus of Nazareth and the Roman Governor Pontius Pilate takes place in Pilate's residence, which is referred to as the Roman Governor's Palace, in Jerusalem on the day before the Jewish Passover in what is now known as the year 33 CE according to the Gregorian calendar. It was witnessed by none other than the Apostle John.

It is evident by its inclusion in John's gospel that He grasped the full importance of the exchange. For John was witnessing the start of a revolution.

Pilate, the governor, was the Roman Empire's representative in Jerusalem, capital of the rebellious province of Palestine. He spent his days tempering an uneasy peace between Caesar, the Emperor, and the Jewish majority of the region. His life was a daily exercise in the compromising of principles and

WHAT IS TRUTH? ON THE NATURE OF EMPIRE

choosing the lesser of evils. Perhaps more than any historical character, Pilate represents the inescapable consequence of humanity orienting itself by the Might makes right mentality and the ever-present fear that it engenders.

Pontius Pilate was the embodiment of Empire.

"Jesus Before Pilate" c. 1890 by Nikolai Ge

In the above exchange, Pilate gives voice to the lament of Empires across the ages: *"What is truth?"*

His reply to Jesus' statement about everyone on the side of truth listening to him (Jesus), *"What is truth?"* is neither a contemptuous mock of Jesus, nor an honest question, rather, it is an exasperated utterance of a man whose life has been reduced to endless compromises, and has seen that the lesser of evils is, in any and every case, necessarily evil.

One must wonder how many heads of state today utter these same words as they contemplate the clear moral law in contrast to what they have been called to do in this life.

How many career military men, after carrying out an assault on the enemy, have grappled with this lament in their souls?

Each of them may grapple, if indeed they pause to reflect on such matters, with a contradiction which has been eloquently expounded by none other than Adin Ballou, who wrote a significant body of work on non-resistance in addition to the *Catechism of Non-Resistance*, in his pamphlet entitled: *"How many Men are Necessary to Change a Crime into a Virtue?"*

"One man may not kill. If he kills a fellow-creature, he is a murderer. If two, ten, a hundred men do so, they, too, are murderers. But a government or a nation may kill as many men as it chooses, and that will not be murder, but a great and noble action. Only gather the people together on a large scale, and a battle of ten thousand men becomes an innocent action. But precisely how many people must there be to make it so?–that is the question. One man cannot plunder and pillage, but a whole nation can. But precisely how many are needed to make it permissible? Why is it that one man, ten, a hundred, may not break the law of God, but a great number may?"

Yeah, it is a contradiction that rightfully haunts thinking persons the world over to this day.

At this flashpoint in history, Pilate speaks for all

WHAT IS TRUTH? ON THE NATURE OF EMPIRE

of them. The Imperial system, which must avail itself to represent the truth in a vain attempt to cloak itself with a shred of legitimacy, leaves its thinking adherents searching in vain for a truth that ultimately relies on the fragile force of arms to perpetuate itself.

On the other side of the truthless void embodied in the person of Pilate, is Jesus of Nazareth, the Messiah. Jesus brought the truth with Him wherever He went. As He stood, soon to be condemned to death by the Empire and the Might makes Right mentality that was swallowing the world, He embodied the truth as never before. John witnessed this moment in the governor's palace and remained shocked to the end of his days.

To Pilate's lament, *"What is truth?"* Jesus replies, then and forevermore: *"God Forgives."*

In doing so, He ratified what he had preached in the Sermon on the Mount, to *"resist not evil,"* what is know today as the doctrine of non-resistance.

Ever since that fateful day, which represents the watershed moment in all of human history, mankind has had the choice to chose the Golden rule, *"Love your neighbor as you love yourself,"* over the self destructive system of Might makes Right. For Jesus represents a clear and permanent change in God's relationship with mankind. God would no longer claim His ultimate authority on the failed Might makes Right ideology, rather, He chose to cleanse the world through Jesus, the ultimate example of non-resistance.

"What Our Lord Saw from the Cross" c.1890 by James Tissot

Jesus' crucifixion served as an indictment to every soul who would claim triumph by defeating others. It served notice of the moral bankruptcy of the Imperial system. For over 2,000 years, those who have stopped at the cross to soak in the message, as John did, have been relentlessly making the world a better place.

In His resurrection, Jesus shattered every excuse that man has for clinging to the failed system of Might makes Right, for to cling to the system is to live in constant search of, or worse, in fear of a truth which has already been revealed. It is to deny that the Empires of this world are perishing and the Kingdom of God is advancing every day.

Mankind, then, has no moral standing when embracing the Might makes right mentality in defense of property and even life. Jesus showed mankind the Better Way, the way to God. Jesus is preparing for us a home in God's Kingdom, where the rule of Empire is vanquished, peace is permanently established, and treasures are secure. For in the Kingdom of God, the Golden Rule reigns as the supreme law of the land.

Yet the true irony and divine beauty of embracing the doctrine of non-resistance here and now is that it serves to enhance both the peace and security of the adherent.

CONCLUSION

As men and women go about their daily occupations, it is relatively common to stop and form an opinion on the benefits or detriments to society of a particular action taken by the government. While it is easy to form an opinion and then take sides of an issue, perhaps the most important question that can be asked is not, "*What should the government do?*" But rather, "*Why should the government get involved?*"

The reason that the second question is rarely if ever asked is that the concept of Empire, or a large scale government which is seen as the ultimate authority, has been part of the human experience for so long that its existence or utility are rarely, if ever, questioned. We pray that this volume has given you the courage to ponder the second question even as a thousand voices around you openly debate the first.

The ignoble goal of all Imperial activities has been to establish and maintain primacy in the affairs of men and women throughout the entire known world. This demand for primacy and allegiance takes the form of the Empire claiming a monopoly on the use of force, which is invariably followed by demands for tribute. Ultimately, the head of Empire will make an appeal to divine right and declare him or herself a deity. As the Empire begins to fade out of existence, it tends to become more violent and less tolerant of dissent, not conscious of the fact that its subjects are increasingly devoting a great deal of their time and energy towards escaping its grasp.

Those who remain within the Empire's grasp are left to either perish at the hands of the Empire or at the hands of those who see no alternative save the use of the force of arms to overthrow the present Imperial leadership, which has been necessarily populated by the members of society who are best able to suppress their conscience in blind pursuit of the Imperial imperatives.

Such is the nature of Empire, and it is lethal to human progress. The Imperial imperative encourages humankind to take the side of Cain who, in the Biblical account related in Genesis chapter 4, led his younger brother, Abel, to a field where he murdered him. Cain's murderous act was born out of the mistaken belief that the removal of others from the earth will secure one's place before God and man. It is an idea that is the driving force behind Imperial action, and it is death.

Fortunately, there is a better way. The Better Way lies neither in violently or peacefully resisting the Empire, it lies in the doctrine of non-resistance, which paradoxically is the best way to ensure one's safety and security regardless of the state of Imperial degeneration that one finds themselves living under.

"Cain leadeth Abel to Death" by James Tissot

However, the path of non-resistance is not without risk, and many of the principle's most noted adherents are noted precisely because they perished while clinging to it.

Adherence to the doctrine of non-resistance is not for the faint of heart, yet it is attainable. The power to embrace the doctrine of non-resistance regardless of peril is found in the person of Jesus of Nazareth, who gave the ultimate reply to the Imperial lament, *"What is truth?"* voiced by Pontius Pilate, who was an instrument of the Roman Empire and the embodiment of the Imperial ideal.

Jesus' response, which is not recorded in the Biblical account but made clear by His subsequent actions, echoes through 2000 years of Imperial rule to guide our actions today:

"God Forgives"

In His reply, we find the power to embrace the doctrine of non-resistance, which is the only hope that mankind has to live in peace both here and now, regardless of the proximity of Imperial rule to his or her daily activities, and in eternity. For to forgive is to live in eternal peace. It is to be in agreement with God himself.

APPENDIX A: THE CATECHISM OF NON-RESISTANCE

The Catechism of Non-Resistance, written by Adin Ballou circa 1846 is presented here in its entirety:

Q. Whence is the word "non-resistance" derived?

A. From the command, "Resist not evil." (M. v. 39.)

Q. What does this word express?

A. It expresses a lofty Christian virtue enjoined on us by Christ.

Q. Ought the word "non-resistance" to be taken in its widest sense–that is to say, as intending that we should not offer any resistance of any kind to evil?

A. No; it ought to be taken in the exact sense of our Saviour's teaching–that is, not repaying evil for evil. We ought to oppose evil by every righteous means in our power, but not by evil.

Q. What is there to show that Christ enjoined non-resistance in that sense?

A. It is shown by the words he uttered at the same time. He said: "Ye have heard, it was said of old, An eye for an eye, and a tooth for a tooth. But I say unto you Resist not evil. But if one smites thee on the right cheek, turn him the other also; and if one will go to law with thee to take thy coat from thee, give him thy cloak also."

Q. Of whom was he speaking in the words, "Ye have heard it was said of old"?

A. Of the patriarchs and the prophets, contained in the Old Testament, which the Hebrews ordinarily call the Law and the Prophets.

Q. What utterances did Christ refer to in the words, "It was said of old"?

A. The utterances of Noah, Moses, and the other prophets, in which they admit the right of doing bodily harm to those who inflict harm, so as to punish and prevent evil deeds.

Q. Quote such utterances.

A. "Whoso sheddeth man's blood, by man shall his blood be shed."–GEN. ix. 6.

"He that smiteth a man, so that he die, shall be surely

put to death...And if any mischief follow, then thou shalt give life for life, eye for eye, tooth for tooth, hand for hand, foot for foot, burning for burning, wound for wound, stripe for stripe." –Ex. xxi. 12 and 23-25.

"He that killeth any man shall surely be put to death. And if a man cause a blemish in his neighbor, as he hath done, so shall it be done unto him: breach for breach, eye for eye, tooth for tooth."–LEV. xxiv. 17, 19, 20.

"Then the judges shall make diligent inquisition; and behold, if the witness be a false witness, and hath testified falsely against his brother, then shall ye do unto him as he had thought to have done unto his brother...And thine eye shall not pity; but life shall go for life, eye for eye, tooth for tooth, hand for hand, foot for foot."–DEUT. xix. 18, 21.

Noah, Moses, and the Prophets taught that he who kills, maims, or injures his neighbors does evil. To resist such evil, and to prevent it, the evil doer must be punished with death, or maiming, or some physical injury. Wrong must be opposed by wrong, murder by murder, injury by injury, evil by evil. Thus taught Noah, Moses, and the Prophets. But Christ rejects all this. "I say unto you," is written in the Gospel, "resist not evil," do not oppose injury with injury, but rather bear repeated injury from the evil doer. What was permitted is forbidden. When we understand what kind of resistance they taught, we know exactly what resistance Christ forbade.

Q. Then the ancients allowed the resistance of injury

WHAT IS TRUTH? ON THE NATURE OF EMPIRE

by injury?

A. Yes. But Jesus forbids it. The Christian has in no case the right to put to death his neighbor who has done him evil, or to do him injury in return.

Q. May he kill or maim him in self-defense?

A. No.

Q. May he go with a complaint to the judge that he who has wronged him may be punished?

A. No. What he does through others, he is in reality doing himself.

Q. Can he fight in conflict with foreign enemies or disturbers of the peace?

A. Certainly not. He cannot take any part in war or in preparations for war. He cannot make use of a deadly weapon. He cannot oppose injury to injury, whether he is alone or with others, either in person or through other people.

Q. Can he voluntarily vote or furnish soldiers for the government?

A. He can do nothing of that kind if he wishes to be faithful to Christ's law.

Q. Can he voluntarily give money to aid a government resting on military force, capital punishment, and violence in general?

A. No, unless the money is destined for some special object, right in itself, and good both in aim and means.

Q. Can he pay taxes to such a government?

A. No; he ought not voluntarily to pay taxes, but he ought not to resist the collecting of taxes. A tax is levied by the government, and is exacted independently of the will of the subject. It is impossible to resist it without having recourse to violence of some kind. Since the Christian cannot employ violence, he is obliged to offer his property at once to the loss by violence inflicted on it by the authorities.

Q. Can a Christian give a vote at elections, or take part in government or law business?

A. No; participation in election, government, or law business is participation in government by force.

Q. Wherein lies the chief significance of the doctrine of non-resistance?

A. In the fact that it alone allows of the possibility of eradicating evil from one's own heart, and also from one's neighbor's. This doctrine forbids doing that whereby evil has endured for ages and multiplied in the world. He who attacks another and injures him, kindles in the other a feeling of hatred, the root of every evil. To injure another because he has injured us, even with the aim of overcoming evil, is doubling the harm for him and for oneself; it is begetting, or at least setting free and inciting, that evil spirit which we should wish to drive out. Satan can never be driven out by Satan. Error can never be corrected by error, and evil cannot be vanquished by evil.

True non-resistance is the only real resistance to evil. It is crushing the serpent's head. It destroys and in the end extirpates the evil feeling.

Q. But if that is the true meaning of the rule of non-resistance, can it always put into practice?

A. It can be put into practice like every virtue enjoined by the law of God. A virtue cannot be practiced in all circumstances without self-sacrifice, privation, suffering, and in extreme cases loss of life itself. But he who esteems life more than fulfilling the will of God is already dead to the only true life. Trying to save his life he loses it. Besides, generally speaking, where non-resistance costs the sacrifice of a single life or of some material welfare, resistance costs a thousand such sacrifices.

Non-resistance is Salvation; Resistance is Ruin.

It is incomparably less dangerous to act justly than unjustly, to submit to injuries than to resist them with violence, less dangerous even in one's relations to the present life. If all men refused to resist evil by evil our world would be happy.

Q. But so long as only a few act thus, what will happen to them?

A. If only one man acted thus, and all the rest agreed to crucify him, would it not be nobler for him to die in the glory of non-resisting love, praying for his enemies, than to live to wear the crown of Caesar stained with the blood of the slain? However, one man, or a thousand men, firmly resolved not to oppose evil by evil are far more free from danger by violence than those who resort to violence, whether among civilized or savage neighbors. The robber, the murderer, and the cheat will leave them in peace, sooner than those who oppose them with arms, and those who take up the sword shall perish by the sword, but those who seek after peace, and behave kindly and harmlessly, forgiving and forgetting injuries, for the most part enjoy peace, or, if they die, they die blessed. In this way, if all kept the ordinance of non-resistance, there would obviously be no evil nor crime. If the majority acted thus they would establish the rule of love and good will even over evil doers, never opposing evil with evil, and never resorting to force. If there were a moderately large minority of such men, they would exercise such a salutary moral influence on society that every cruel punishment would be abolished, and violence and feud would be replaced by peace and love. Even if there were only a small minority of them, they would rarely experience anything worse than the world's contempt, and meantime the world, though unconscious of it, and not grateful for it, would be continually becoming wiser and better for their unseen action on it. And if in the worst case some members of the minority were persecuted to death, in dying for the truth they would have left behind them their doctrine, sanctified by the blood of their martyrdom. Peace, then, to all who seek peace, and may overruling love be the imperishable heritage of every soul who obeys willingly Christ's word, "Resist not evil."

ADIN BALLOU.

WHAT IS MONEY?

A quest to answer the question of the ages

Volume II

DAVID MINT

WHAT IS MONEY? A QUEST TO ANSWER THE QUESTION OF THE AGES

VOLUME II

CONTENTS

Introduction	79
What is Money?	81
Our Journey	83
The Troubling Quest	86
The Obvious Answer	89
Conclusion	94

INTRODUCTION

What is money? It seems such a simple question, one that is scarcely worth asking. Everyone knows that money is money, you either have it or you don't. It goes by various names, dollars, Benjamins, wampum, pesos, yen, quid, euros, Yuan, rupees, rubles, and most humans will spend their entire adult lives trying to earn or beg enough of it to give to those who demand money from them in exchange for something. Some will have money left over when they take their final breath; some will take their last breath a net debtor, leaving their unhappy creditors behind.

In a sense, much of one's adult life is spent gathering and protecting what they believe to be money. Given the inordinate amount of time spent by humans trying to obtain money, is it sufficient to simply define it by the name of a national currency or a slang derivative of the official name? The premise of this book is that it is not, for the ability to correctly answer the question, *What is Money?*, may not only mark the difference between taking one's last breath on the debtor's or creditor's side of the ledger, it could determine the very fate of mankind.

Beginning from this premise, we seek to gain an understanding of and form a working definition of money that will help the reader not only enrich themselves, but at the same time, enrich the human race and the planet that we have been entrusted with.

While the benefits of such an understanding are tremendous, we are compelled to advise you, dear reader, that you are about to cross the Rubicon, and you may never again be able to view your paystub or bank statements in the same light.

This will serve as your final warning. If you prefer to take the blue pill, you may stop reading now. Your paystub and bank statement will look exactly the same as they did before you opened these pages. However, if you take the red pill and read on, we'll guide you to as complete of an understanding of what money is as has been given to man.

WHAT IS MONEY?

As you choke down the red pill, we will begin to expound on that eternally important question that few people have bothered to ask, save once, likely around the tender age of four. When the eternally important question, "*What is Money?*" was posed by that inquisitive four year old, most parents gave them exactly the same answer that their parents had given them when they dared ask the question at four years of age, the name of the national currency. Then, once the parents provided proof of the answer to the skeptical four year old in the form of coins and bills, the question had been settled for life.

Is the name of the national currency a satisfactory answer to the inquisitive four year olds inquiry? On the surface, it would appear to be. However, if one stops to ponder this answer, they will quickly see that what appeared to be a straightforward answer is but a thin veil over a troubling circular reasoning that goes something like this: "*Why is this piece of paper money? Because *everybody says it is."* Like any thinly veiled circular reasoning, it depends upon the finicky, yet moldable, human psyche to perpetuate itself. This dependence on self-perpetuation leads to the inescapable fact that the US Dollar will continue to be money in the United States, in our chosen national currency example...until it is not.

At this point, you may be thinking to yourself, *"don't legal tender laws dictate what money is?"* It is a worthy question. However, the response, unfortunately, leads down the same rabbit hole of circular reasoning. Legal tender laws will dictate that the US Dollar is money in the United States...until they don't. Again, as is the case with man-made legislation, it is subject to the finicky human psyche to perpetuate itself.

We are now leaving the comfortable place of thinking that we knew what money was, to having to define something that we once took for granted. I do not blame you, dear reader, if you are content with the answer that you had slept comfortably at night knowing all of your life. To grapple with this question is to question many things that have been taken for granted. It can be an unsettling experience. Before we move further, we wish to share with you the series of events that lead us to discover the red pill. We pray that this brief pause will give you ample time to calm your nerves and ease you in to what comes next.

OUR JOURNEY

We were first unsettled by this unpleasant question during a class on monetary policy at the Universitat de Barcelona in the spring of 2004, during our MBA studies. In the opening class session, the female professor, a regal, executive type, held up a small jar full of shredded greenish paper and asked the class if we knew what was inside. The unsettling answer was that the jar had been filled with $50,000 worth of Federal Reserve Notes that had been removed from circulation and destroyed. Simple enough, right? As dollar bills circulate to the point of disintegration, the monetary authority must take action to replace them. The professor used this visual aid to nail home the point that what most of us use as money does not exist in a real, tangible sense, rather, it is an invention created to meet the policy demands of the fiscal and monetary authorities. An invention, it turns out that can be created and destroyed at whim.

We were taken aback and struggled to catch our

breath. While at the time our Castilian Spanish, the language that the class was being taught in, was still a bit shaky, we were certain that we had grasped what the professor had said, and our head began to spin at the implications.

She went on to explain that corporations and, at base, all forms of for profit businesses are simply money machines which strive to minimize money inputs and maximize money outputs. The difference between the inputs and outputs is what is known as profit. This is obvious enough and it was logical that she would share this insight with our MBA class, which was being trained to manage said corporations.

At this point, as we were nearing comprehension, something short circuited in our mind as we attempted to reconcile the logic of corporations across the planet existing for the purpose of creating money and then seeing that same money end up shredded and destroyed in rather large quantities. Surely there was some sort of gatekeeper, ensuring that a replica replaced every shredded bill, maintaining the pedigree of the herd, so to speak, right?

At that point, we couldn't think, the motor of our mind had seized up to the point that we missed nearly every question that day on a pop quiz that tested our knowledge on proper reactions, in terms of monetary policy, to various economic data. Each question required but a simple answer. Given the economic data presented, should one move to increase or decrease the money supply? Simple probability should have allowed us to answer at least half of the questions right. However, as the

WHAT IS MONEY? A QUEST TO ANSWER THE QUESTION OF THE AGES

professor read off the answers, we realized that any questions we had answered correctly were primarily due to our misunderstanding the question (as we stated above, we were still learning Castilian Spanish, as well as Catalan) rather than any sort of grasp we possessed of generally accepted policy remedies.

In retrospect, that day was the day that completely changed the way in which we viewed US Dollars, euros, and all other centrally managed currencies of the world. You see, we were answering all of the questions about monetary policy with the assumption that the monetary authorities wanted to maintain the quantity and, by extension, the value of the currency that they were managing. As our results on the quiz reflected, we were dead wrong.

As we sipped a coffee at the café afterwards, slowly regaining our mental capacities, our focus turned to the motives of the monetary authorities that so dutifully printed and shredded the bits of paper we had assumed were money ever since the tender age of four, when we first ventured the question. If monetary authorities are not trying to maintain the value of these currencies, what on earth are they trying to do?

THE TROUBLING QUEST

As you can see, our quest to define money has taken us farther and perhaps troubled us further than many would have imagined. Should this come as a surprise? The subject of money is generally taken lightly because to ponder it deeply can be deeply troubling. However, in pondering it we find we are in good company.

None other than Jesus of Nazareth, during his earthly ministry, talked about money more than any other subject with the exception of the Kingdom of God.

"For where your treasure is, there your heart will be also."

If hearing from the Son of God on the subject is not persuasive, consider the following comments attributed to Robert H. Hemphill, an insightful credit manager at the Federal Reserve Bank of Atlanta during the 1930's:

WHAT IS MONEY? A QUEST TO ANSWER THE QUESTION OF THE AGES

"Money is the most important subject intellectual persons can investigate and reflect upon. It is so important that our present civilization may collapse unless it is widely understood and its defects remedied very soon."

If a credit manager for a Federal Reserve Bank, the current curators of what the most persons in United States of America, indeed the world, deem to be money was concerned about its defects, and some 80 years later we find ourselves using the same defective money on a scale that would have caused Mr. Hemphill to soil himself, this should be cause for alarm. However, if the Son of God and the soiled Mr. Hemphill can be so easily brushed off, perhaps the famous economist John Maynard Keynes' dramatic statement about the consequences of currency debasement, which he eloquently calls *"debauching,"* will serve to finally set off the alarm bells:

"Lenin is certainly right. There is no subtler or more severe means of overturning the existing basis of society than to debauch the currency. The process engages all the hidden forces of economic law on the side of destruction, and it does it in a manner which not one man in a million is able to diagnose."

Yes, Keynes is referring to Vladimir Lenin, the leader of the Bolshevik party who gave the Russian people the October Revolution and the Red Terror, among other things.

After having our faith in paper currency shaken

in Barcelona, we moved to Portland, Oregon and landed a job. For the first time we could remember, we, like the global corporate money machines, were running a personal operating surplus on a regular basis. The year was 2006, and somehow we were uncomfortable about the stock market and home ownership as wise investments for our operating surplus. We were also skeptical at the prospect of simply keeping our savings in a bank account, as the image of the shredded dollar bills in the jar haunted us still. What to do? The dilemma, which we now understand is common to man, drove us to search for what, in retrospect, was the obvious answer to the question at hand, "*What is Money?*"

THE OBVIOUS ANSWER

We are now returning to the question, *What is Money?* First and foremost, we must understand that money is a concept. As such, the term money, in its purest sense, cannot be permanently affixed to any object. The concept of money is the collectively held belief that something possesses certain attributes that make it suitable to serve as money. In order to understand this concept, we must start by defining the specific attributes that cause an otherwise innate object to be crowned as money, or, to translate this idea into precise economic terminology, what is it that causes the coveted monetary premium to attach itself to a particular object.

What are the attributes that something must possess to be used as money? To answer this question, we will paraphrase a list that was compiled by Jason Hommel. The list includes the following attributes that something must possess to meet most people's criteria of money. While Mr. Hommel expands upon these attributes extensively in his writings, we content ourselves to define each attribute by posing a simple question, which, may we add, is a brilliant and all too seldom employed literary and educational device.

The attributes of money, then, are the following:

First, it should operate as a *medium of exchange*. Will other people accept this item in trade for something else?

Second, it should operate as a *unit of account*. Can the item be easily divided without destroying its value?

Third, it should be a *reliable store of value*. Will the item purchase the same amount of goods in ten, twenty, or three thousand years from now as it will today?

And **fourth**, it should be *anonymous*. Can the item be freely transferred amongst parties?

The concept of money is so basic and yet so indispensable to the human experience that misconceptions surrounding money, once they are embedded in the collective psyche (which for most of us occurred at four years of age, give or take a year), can persist for a very long time. In fact, the concept of money is so deeply embedded that people, acting as a collective, will continue to use an item as money, even when that item ceases to possess the attributes listed above, until the whole of society comes to a new tacit agreement as to what constitutes money in trade.

For continuing to use bad money, our name for items which act as money but do not possess the above attributes, is, more often than not, tacitly deemed preferable to making the collective switch to good money, despite its proven benefits and a clear preference on the part of individuals to hold good money. Additionally, government action, via the passage of legal tender laws or other decrees that mandate what money is, may further perpetuate the use of bad money in a society.

Despite an individual preference to receive payments in good money, individuals, once they are able to make the distinction, will attempt to make payments to others in bad money until such time that the bad money in circulation is summarily rejected. This phenomenon is known as Gresham's Law:

"When a government compulsorily overvalues one type of money and undervalues another, the undervalued money will leave the country or disappear from circulation into hoards, while the overvalued money will flood into circulation."

As Gresham's Law suggests, the increased use of bad money is a phenomenon that is perpetuated by government authorities. Private individuals who are able to make the distinction between good money and bad money, as you are about to become by virtue of choosing to take the red pill, will begin to hold good money and circulate the bad like a hot potato once they are able to recognize the bad money for what it is.

However, the society that is obliged to continue circulating the bad money will do so until the bad money self destructs like a secret message sent between spies. The reason for the collective denial, both on the part of the people and the government, is simple. While a change to good money promises innumerable benefits, these benefits do not become apparent until the society begins to clear the rubble of the economic collapse caused by the long term circulation of the bad money. Sensing the pain to come, the society will tacitly decide to put off the day of reckoning until the monetary change is thrust upon them by necessity. The change occurs when the shortage of goods in the real world becomes so intense that the bad money is categorically rejected in exchange for them.

So what item or items in the world today possess the four attributes of money? After reviewing the four attributes presented above, as well as reviewing all of known human history, we can conclude that, in an overwhelming majority of cases, precious and at times base metals, namely gold, silver, and copper, have proven to be best suited to serve mankind in the role of money. As a medium of exchange, they are universally recognized. As a unit of account, they are divisible without destroying their content. As a store of value, gold and silver are not easily pulled from the ground and coined for use, and in this sense, they cannot be easily devalued through the sudden creation of additional units. Finally, in terms of anonymity, they can be freely transferred without passing identifiable information regarding the parties to a transaction along with them. This final detail virtually eliminates the risk of modern day financial fraud.

Bear in mind that on the earth there is no perfect item or element that can be said to possess the four attributes of money in perfect measure. Money is an economic good, and whatever element or item that is crowned as money by a society must be constantly checked by Adam Smith's invisible hand of the market to ensure that supply and demand are ever tending towards balance. That said, precious metals, specifically gold and silver, have consistently throughout human history been found to be the natural elements best suited to physically embody the concept of money on every continent by all peoples who engage in trade.

CONCLUSION

The root cause of the modern financial crises is the widespread misconception as to what is best suited to assume the role of money in trade. The root of this misconception is a lack of a conscious understanding of the concept of money. Money plays such a vital role in society that most assume that what we currently use as money falls into the category of good money. However, a review of the above attributes and a peek at the quotes from Jesus of Nazareth, the now soiled Robert H. Hemphill, and John Maynard Keynes starkly illustrate that our understanding of money is lacking.

The fact is that ever since August 15, 1971, the world has circulated what we would now label as bad money, in trade. For on that fateful day, then President Richard Nixon closed the window on gold convertibility of the US dollar. Ever since then, Federal Reserve Notes, which at their base are debt instruments, have tacitly and almost seamlessly occupied the place of gold as the cornerstone of the

WHAT IS MONEY? A QUEST TO ANSWER THE QUESTION OF THE AGES

world's monetary system.

On that day in 1971, Nixon effectively replaced gold, which we have identified, along with silver, as most nearly possessing the attributes of good money, with what amounts to nothing more than a glorified IOU. Since 1971, the US Dollar has been a mere invention of man, and it has maintained its status as money largely via fiat, the dictate of a ruler.

Money created via fiat has an infallible track record in the following sense: In 100% of live experiments, money created by fiat has failed in spectacular fashion, with catastrophic effects for those unfortunate enough to have placed their faith in it. We are currently nearly 42 years into the largest experiment with money created via fiat that the world has ever known. The disaster that awaits mankind when this experiment ends the same way that all of the other fiat experiments have ended simply boggles the mind.

Fortunately you and I, by virtue of choosing the red pill, can return to using gold and silver as money here and now. The choice to use gold and silver as money has numerous positive side effects for the overall well being of every single person on the planet, as well as for the planet itself. The most notable and perhaps the basis for all of the other healthy side effects is the tacit and universal incentive to create and conserve physical capital. This phenomenon, which in economic parlance is known as capital formation, is what allowed mankind to claw out of the feudal age and prosper in ways that were unimaginable just a century ago, and it is what will allow mankind to collectively and peacefully enjoy a future where anything is possible.

OF MONEY AND METALS

The Operation of a Free Money Supply Explained

Volume III

OF MONEY AND METALS: THE OPERATION OF A FREE MONEY SUPPLY EXPLAINED

VOLUME III

CONTENTS

Balance: An Introduction	99
The Keynesian Nightmare	101
Debt: The Barbarous Relic	105
The Operation of a Free Money Supply Explained	110
Free Money Refutes Gresham's Law	114
Conclusion	118
Epilogue: Is Fiduciary Money Really Money or Cleverly Disguised Debt?	122
Are Bitcoins Money? The Concept of Digital Currency and the Desperate Need for a Free Money Supply	131

BALANCE: AN INTRODUCTION

We have observed that there is a perfect balance in God's creation. Some call it a yin and yang, male and female, mercy and justice, freedom and slavery, heat and cold. For every extreme, there is a force which, given enough time, will work to counteract the excesses wrought by the seemingly uninhibited operation of its polar opposite.

It should come as no surprise, then, that in the economic sphere, debt and money fall into the same category of opposing natural forces. One takes from the future to provide for the present, the other takes from the past towards the same end.

Simple, right? Male, Female, Yin, Yang, case closed.

Yet circa 2013, for some odd reason, there seems to be an abundance of debt and a dearth of money in the world. The world as we know it is perilously out of balance.

How can this be? Why are things so far out of balance? We will sum up what is otherwise a long and painful explanation in the following way: Roughly 100 years ago, by decree of the financial authorities, debt was declared to be money. Ever since then, mankind has lived in a state of economic confusion.

On one hand, mankind has seen an unprecedented level of technological advances and a resulting rise in his standard of living. On the other hand, on net, he, or someone acting in his name, has borrowed an unprecedented amount of money from the future in order to achieve these advances and consequent rise in his living standards.

How is this possible? Didn't simply declaring that debt is money relieve man of having to save? After all, if everyone simply assents to accepting promises to pay in the future for goods or services which are delivered or performed today, has not humanity trumped the need for savings, the Yang, as it were?

More to the point, have the laws of nature with regards to money been permanently suspended or altered?

If only it were so. Unfortunately, the longer mankind labors under the false assumption that debt is money, the greater his pain will be as nature takes it upon itself to unilaterally bring the earth into balance.

THE KEYNESIAN NIGHTMARE

In 1913 the US Congress passed the now infamous Federal Reserve act. Not unlike the recent passage of the 2012 National Defense Authorization Act, it happened during the winter holiday when the populace was largely distracted by the many and varied festivities of the season.

While the Federal Reserve act has wrought many injustices on the earth, undoubtedly the greatest injustice that continues to cause the greatest amount of damage to mankind was the subtle replacement of money proper with Federal Reserve notes. This action effectively declared that debt is money in direct violation of natural law.

While this fact may have seemed like a minor detail with regards to custodianship at the time, the declaration was, tantamount to handing over of Bilbo's One Ring to the financial and governmental authorities of the earth. For it gave them largely unfettered access to the accumulated savings of the entire earth and, in the case that the savings ran dry, the unhindered ability to incur debts against the future production of the entire earth as well.

The only thing that they needed was to compel the entire earth to accept debts as money in everyday exchange. Today, circa 2013, they have largely succeeded in compelling both Eastern and Western Civilizations to accept debts as money through a variety of both pacific and at times violent means.

Yet as we stated earlier, debt and money are polar opposites. To declare that debt is money was not only insane; it is a direct violation of natural law. This violation of natural law began to reap its terrible harvest in 1933 with the onset of the great depression. Yet instead of admitting defeat and leaving the decision as to the proper quantities of debt and money in the hands of the people, where it naturally belongs, the authorities presented an academic apologist to confirm for them that debt was indeed now money and that all that was required was more of it.

Enter John Maynard Keynes, a British economist best known as the father of the Keynesian school of economic thought. Mr. Keynes developed a thesis that diagnosed the economic problem facing the earth as a lack of money. While his thesis was, at base, correct, the declaration of debt as money had created a catch 22 that hinders policy makers to this day. What Keynes and those who subscribed to his theories failed to realize is that the Federal Reserve, in declaring that debt was money, had placed a significant impediment to the creation of money, the remedy that the earth so desperately needed.

Instead, Keynes and his colleagues skipped over

OF MONEY AND METALS: THE OPERATION OF A FREE MONEY SUPPLY EXPLAINED

the only viable solution, namely, allowing the free market to determine what constitutes debt and money, and offered the world a solution which has been the equivalent of injecting poison directly into the veins of the ailing economy. The poison of which we speak was injected as a result of a test of the following erroneous hypothesis:

"The problem is that there is not enough money. Because debt is now money, it follows that more debt must be incurred to create the money necessary to spur production, employment, and all the things that people now associate with a healthy economy. Further, there is not enough money precisely because the people are not sufficiently indebting themselves. Since the people are not inclined to further indebt themselves, it is the duty of the government to increase overall indebtedness, and therefore the money supply, on behalf of the people. It must force the people to do what they cannot (or more accurately, will not) do for themselves."

*{**Editor's note:** When people are reducing debt, the people are in fact reacting to the demands of natural law, which under the circumstances is calling for less debt and more saving for the economy to achieve balance}*

As insane as this line of thought sounds, it is today generally accepted as natural law by nearly every Harvard trained economist, and therefore nearly every government and central bank official, on the planet. The only difference between the 1930's and today is that today, circa 2013, this disastrous line of thought is now practiced on a much grander scale and, given the accumulated imbalances of 100 years of misguided economic activity, the stakes are now infinitely higher.

DEBT: THE BARBAROUS RELIC

As the world descended further into depression which eventually led it into the Second World War *{**Editor's Note:** It should come as no surprise that the only two World Wars have come after the declaration that debt is money}*, The Keynesian adherents clamored for more debt as it seemed, under their hypothesis, the only viable answer to the world's economic ills.

What Keynes and his Harvard trained legions fail to comprehend is that the only permanent cure for an economic depression is to allow each individual to declare what he or she will use as money and allow market participants to tacitly coalesce around what, at that point in time, is best suited for the role of money. For balance sheet recessions, such as the one the world is currently experimenting, are merely symptoms of a rigid money supply that has failed to keep up with the demands of a dynamic economy.

Under current theory, the government sacrifices the dynamic economy in the name of preserving the "integrity" (we use the term here in jest) of the monetary system.

When it is quite obvious that it is the monetary system itself, and not the economy, that has failed, the government's response of forcing debt creation can only be seen as idiotic at best and more accurately hostile to economic activity.

What makes the situation of the past 100 years even more untenable is that money, instead of operating as a lubricant for economic activity, which is its natural role, is operating like concrete filling the delicate engine of the economy. Such is the inherently destructive nature of debt as money.

For the only rule with regards to money that is imposed as a matter of natural law is that debt cannot ever be money. It is a concept so clear that it escapes not only most academics and government officials, but also many in the general population.

Now, the Keynesian indoctrinated readers of these words are no doubt dusting off the silver bullet of Keynesian theory: That gold, which is widely held by gold bugs and old money types alike as the logical alternative to the debt-is-money insanity, is nothing more than a barbarous relic. In layman's terms, Keynesian theory holds that any attempt to limit the money supply via natural means, the most popular being a gold standard (fixing the price of gold in terms of monetary units) will cause a deflationary spiral that will bankrupt the entire world.

Even Adam Smith, the father of modern economics, argued that the mining of metals for use as currency was essentially a lamentable waste of resources.

OF MONEY AND METALS: THE OPERATION OF A FREE MONEY SUPPLY EXPLAINED

We could not agree with them more. The limited amounts of gold in the world make it wholly unfit for everyday exchange. Gold, rather, is generally agreed upon to be the most perfect savings vehicle that the world has yet discovered.

So Keynes, despite promoting a theory that sacrifices the Yang (savings) and glorifies the Yin (debt) is right after all? Not quite...

Using the same logic with which the Keynesian so adeptly slays the gold standard, it quickly becomes obvious that by declaring that debt is money is not only a violation of natural law, it makes debt, rather than gold, the new barbarous relic for the very reason that debt has essentially replaced gold as the basis of the money supply. However, if gold had its flaws in terms of quantitative limitations, debt as a currency base possesses a design flaw that can only be described as catastrophic.

Debt, as the basis of the money supply, has a distinct disadvantage to gold in that debt, unlike gold, can be quickly and completely destroyed. Once it is assumed by the majority that a certain debtor will not be able to make good on their debts, the debts owed by the debtor, and any money in circulation which is either directly or indirectly related to the existence of these debts, is destroyed. For debt, at its base level, is a figment of the imagination until it is settled in real terms by the delivery of money in settlement of the debt.

It would hold, then, that debt, the new barbarous relic, is infinitely more dangerous than gold when used as money. The reasoning is the following, while the quantity of debt in the world can be suddenly and permanently reduced, the quantity of gold, which is admittedly difficult to increase, is at the same time extremely difficult to decrease.

Yet, even given the strong advantage of gold over debt as money, it is obvious that Keynesians as well as gold bugs are terribly misguided in formulating their ultimate solution to the eternal problem of the money supply.

When it comes to determining the proper money supply, Adam Smith's invisible hand of the market can be seen slapping both Keynesians and gold bugs silly!

For the problem with declaring anything, be it gold, debt, or white elephants as money, has nothing to do with the fitness of gold, debt, or white elephants for use as money, rather, the problem lies in the act of a minority attempting to dictate what the majority will use as money.

Money, in a general sense, is a good of the highest order. There is nothing in nature that states that gold, silver, seashells, or anything else must be used as money. The historical association of gold and silver as money is the result of their superior fitness for the role of money. It is simply a product of the collective wisdom of mankind, gleaned from experience as free exchange and the division of labor began to bring order to man's chaotic surroundings.

However, just because gold and silver have proven their superiority in their role as money in the past, does not necessarily mean that they enjoy some sort of divine designation as money.

Gold and silver, like all things occurring in nature, are in limited supply. The fact that they occur in nature gives them a distinct advantage over

OF MONEY AND METALS: THE OPERATION OF A FREE MONEY SUPPLY EXPLAINED

debt, which, at its base, is simply a promise to pay in the future. Debt, though it can disappear in an instant, is theoretically in infinite supply. There is never a shortage of persons or entities that will accept goods today in exchange for offering a promise to pay at a future date. As such, debt will quickly lose value against scarce real goods due to the fact that debt, again in theory, enjoys an infinite supply.

Anyone can make promises to pay in the future; it is the function of debt markets to determine what those promises are worth today. Ironically, the value of debt today is perilously tied to speculations about the money supply, which is, in turn, dependent upon the issuance of debt. Thus, declaring debt as money provides the economy with yet another hindrance in that the debt markets are increasingly disconnected from their noble origins; the debtor's perceived productive capacity.

It is clear that mankind is in a perilous predicament. Will we take hold of the simple answer, which lies in free banking and free determination of what will serve as money?

THE OPERATION OF A FREE MONEY SUPPLY EXPLAINED

Natural law is always operating, always demanding a balance of accounts in the real world, not simply on an accountant's ledger or numbers on a bank statement.

It is then foolishness for anyone to assume that a central authority, no matter how clairvoyant, can properly estimate the money supply necessary for human economic activity to continue at the optimal rate, balancing both the quantity of debt and money to provide for both present and future wants and needs using all of the information which is collectively available.

It is for this reason that it is imperative that people be free to decide for themselves both what will serve as money as well as its value in exchange. History has shown that people do not need to be guided in these matters, for the need for money as a means of exchange is so expedient that market participants will tacitly come to a decision as to both

OF MONEY AND METALS: THE OPERATION OF A FREE MONEY SUPPLY EXPLAINED

what will serve as money and what the present value of said money is.

History has shown that, if people tacitly chose gold or anything natural as money, economic activity and the resulting benefits to society will accumulate so rapidly that the natural limitations on the supply of gold or other chosen element will quickly act as a constraint. If gold, or anything else is declared money by decree, this supply limitation quickly becomes a problem.

However, if the majority has simply chosen gold for use as money, the same majority will quickly and tacitly gravitate to a secondary natural source of money with which to augment the primary natural money supply. Historically, this secondary source of money has been silver. The invisible hand of the market (Adam Smith's moniker for the tacit, active balancing of the forces of supply and demand), if left to its own devices, will naturally set the exchange rate between the previous monetary medium, in this case gold, and the new medium, in this case silver.

Once economic activity further accelerates and the benefits continue to accrue to a larger portion of the population, the supply of silver will predictably act as a natural restraint. Again, if left to their own devices, the majority will quickly and tacitly adopt another item occurring in nature to be used as money. Historically, this third source has been copper. Once again, the invisible hand of the market will work to set a natural exchange rate for the new monetary medium against the existing monetary mediums.

Yet even the supply of copper, abundant as it may be, will eventually serve as a restraint, and so on, and so forth. Eventually, in this example of what we like to call the operation of a free money supply, gold will tend to operate as a form of savings and settlement only in the largest of transactions, with silver serving as money at an intermediate level while copper would be the most widely circulated currency for smaller transactions.

The beauty of free money is that, should the supply of copper become a constraint, steel, nickel, or some other more abundant natural resource will take the place of copper for use in smaller transactions, and so on, so that the money supply, in a general sense, will always be perfectly suited for the rate of economic activity which is occurring.

It is important to note that, while history has shown a preference for metals to be used as money, in the free money (and by extension, free banking) theory there is no requirement that a metallic substance be adopted as money. In fact, money can be anything that those participating in exchange bilaterally accept as payment for goods and settlement of debts. As you will recall, the only thing that money should not be, by definition, is debt.

While it is obvious that debt can be exchanged in the place of money for a time, as the past 100 years have shown us, common sense, logic, and natural law will demand that the debts that circulate eventually be settled in real terms. The creation of debt as money severely distorts economic reality and, the greater the quantity of debt that is created, the greater the demanded settlement in real terms will be, regardless of how many times one chants the Keynesian mantra recently made famous once again

OF MONEY AND METALS: THE OPERATION OF A FREE MONEY SUPPLY EXPLAINED

by former Vice President of the US Dick Cheney *"Deficits don't matter."*

The superiority of free money is that the money supply is free to adapt to the natural pace of economic activity, which is nothing more than an expression of the changing wants and needs of consumers. If the principle of free money is allowed to operate, the money supply will not be hindered by unnatural constraints which have nothing to do with economic reality and are imposed by what is, at best, an uninformed or disinterested or, at worst, a malicious monetary authority.

The current debt as money system, far from providing a perfectly elastic money supply, has created the economic equivalent of concrete, which is now hardening inside the engine of economy, instead of providing it with much needed lubrication. If this insanity carries on much longer, the engine known as the economy will be shattered as economic reality begins to take a jackhammer to it.

For the only thing certain is that the economic imbalances that currently exist will be brought into balance. The indomitable operation of natural law demands it.

FREE MONEY REFUTES GRESHAM'S LAW

The principle of free money also renders null and void any arguments as to what constitutes good or bad money, for this determination will be made on a daily basis by producers and consumers rather than a monetary authority who is acting on mere theory with severely limited data.

Absent a government declaration of what is money and how much said money is worth, there is no longer bad money driving out good money, as Gresham's Law so perceptively observes, as the only way bad money can come into existence is via a government decree which sets the value of an item declared to be money at a higher rate than the item's natural value in the marketplace. What remains, then, as the ultimate determinant of what is money and how much it is worth are the two parties to a transaction, who are generally in the best position to determine such matters.

OF MONEY AND METALS: THE OPERATION OF A FREE MONEY SUPPLY EXPLAINED

"But this would destroy exchange as we know it!" comes the cry from apologists of legal tender laws. *"No one will know what anything is worth, let alone how to pay for it!"*

On the contrary, the free operation of the money supply would, by necessity, cause everyone engaging in exchange to be acutely aware of both what constitutes money and how much it is worth. It is legal tender laws that serve to pull the wool over everyone's eyes as to the true value of money. It is legal tender laws, which have no place in the free money economy. It is legal tender laws that give rise to the bad money, which, according to the operation of Gresham's law, will be passed between parties in exchange like a hot potato.

When seen through a different lens, that of the free operation of the money supply, the absurdity of legal tender laws becomes clear. Commodity (or free) money is unhindered by the artificial restraint of existing debts and is constrained only by the productive will of society. Commodity (free) money is free to accurately reflect the price of goods and services in light of the perceived existing supply and productive capacity of both the good being offered in exchange and the good offered in payment, commonly known as money.

Money, as most people instinctively understand it, is simply an ordinary good whose utility and value are greatly enhanced by its wide acceptance in trade. This value enhancement is known as the monetary premium that is attached to the value of a good or commodity. If one strives to remove the cost of producing money, as Adam Smith so nobly aspired to do, it is clear that the best way to do this is to allow the good which is acting as money to be produced in the most efficient way by the greatest number of artisans as are necessary to fulfill the present demand for money.

But how would all of these artisans, blindly creating all of this commodity money, know when to stop producing were it not for legal tender laws or centralized monetary authorities?

Here, there is no risk of oversimplifying the answer, for the answer is painfully simple. As persons competing in the free market who have chosen to produce money, they are likely to be the first to know when there is too much money in circulation, for their orders for new money will uncannily drop when the economy has enough money to function efficiently.

Further, any commodity that is only marginally used in the production of money will quickly and smoothly have its supply directed to other, more efficient uses as the incentive (read the realized margin or monetary premium) to use it as money is incrementally reduced as supply begins to overtake demand. Each producer is therefore free to choose his or her exit point from the market.

Take the case of copper. If copper becomes monetized by the free will of the participants in the economy, it stands to reason that it could be demonetized by the same free market operation. Should economic activity slow to the point where the pace of saving and exchange no longer calls for copper to assume a role as money, as copper is demonetized, those holding copper may find it preferable to melt the copper that they have in

OF MONEY AND METALS: THE OPERATION OF A FREE MONEY SUPPLY EXPLAINED

monetary form and sell it as a consumer good. In this sense, the operation of free money allows all actors in the economy to determine their own exit point.

The process of demonetization is simply a matter or free choice when something that occurs in nature is used as money. It first moves to the fringes of use as money, as a Jeton or modern day casino chip is used in place of money. In time, the material will be demonetized completely.

Such is the operation of the free money supply. While fluid changes in what acts as money and the constantly changing exchange rates may at first appear to be an unattractive side effect when dealing with something that is indispensible to most people's day to day existence as money is, it is these very qualities of the free money principle that make it superior in every way to a centrally managed money supply.

CONCLUSION

This volume has been presented for your consideration with two purposes in mind. Its first purpose is to expose the catastrophic shortcomings of declaring that debt is money. The declaration of debt as money is a dangerous violation of natural law and has thrown the world out of balance in ways that were never before possible.

The second, and more important purpose is to debunk the fallacy that a metal-based monetary system is doomed to deflation. This is the fallacy that gave rise to the idea that debt could better serve as money in the first place. History has shown that gold, silver, copper, and more recently nickel and steel have all taken on the role of money seamlessly as the need arose.

Monetary units, similar to the people that use it, work best when they are free. Money, as an economic good, works fastest most efficiently when it is simply seen as a good of the highest order.

While it is clear today, circa 2013, that the world

OF MONEY AND METALS: THE OPERATION OF A FREE MONEY SUPPLY EXPLAINED

economy is struggling to address fundamental problems, there have been few proposed policy solutions that do not ultimately require the creation of more money and, by default, more debt.

What is widely ignored today by the world's economic experts is that by declaring that debt is money nearly a century ago, the world did not free itself from the constraints on the supply of money set upon it by adherence to a gold standard, rather, it removed the handcuffs of the gold standard and stepped waist deep into a pit filled with fresh concrete.

The only way out of the monetary pit that the economy has fallen into is to allow the peoples of the world to tacitly determine what to use as money. They must be allowed to determine both the form and the quantity of monetary units in a fluid and unhindered manner. The operation of the principle of free money is the only way to ensure that the money supply maintains the proper elasticity through the natural operation of market forces.

Debt, when used as money, enjoys no such elasticity. By necessity, when debt is forced into a role as money, it causes an unnatural proliferation of credit, so that when the inverse of Gresham's law begins to operate (good credits push bad credits out of circulation) the unnatural restriction on the money supply assures that even the best of credits will go bad, and the money supply along with them.

Further, when debt is forcefully demonetized, which is the only way that it can be demonetized under the current regime of legal tender law, the result is more often than not a severe hyperinflation followed by war.

Legal tender laws, such as the modern laws that declare that debt is money, are futile at best and generally destructive. They do, however, permit a small group to reap the monetary margin, or premium, that the artificial monopoly on money creation allows them for a time.

Accepting that an inanimate object is no longer worth what one thought it was can be disappointing, but at least one still has said inanimate object. In the case of debt, accepting that someone cannot deliver what they promised tends to create feelings of resentment and remorse that, depending upon the size of the failure, can lead to violence.

Soon, the world will learn that using debt as money is a dangerous violation of the very laws of nature. As with any violation of natural law, the consequences may be withheld for a time, but they are never avoided. The longer they are artificially withheld, the more swiftly and severely the consequences will be meted out when they can no longer be repressed.

For no man, or group of men, regardless of their number, clairvoyance, or special powers they profess to have, can suspend or accelerate the operation of natural law. The Creator alone reserves that power for himself.

There is a perfect balance in God's creation. Yin and Yang, Male and Female, mercy and justice, heat and cold, money and debt. Calling one extreme the by the name of other is futile and leads only to confusion and destruction.

The time has come to call things at they are. The sooner that the debt which currently circulates in the place of money is called by its real name, the sooner mankind can work to bring its many and varied activities back into harmony with the earth and the incessant demands of natural law.

EPILOGUE

*{**Editor's Note:** The following is an introduction and redaction of an real interaction between the author, who is decidedly not an Ivy League trained economist, and an Ivy League trained economist regarding the nature of fiduciary money. The interaction took place on April 30, 2012}*

Is Fiduciary Money Really Money or Cleverly Disguised Debt? The Mint Educates an Ivy League Trained Economist

These are smart people, no doubt, the money managers and central bankers involved in the debacle that is the western financial system, circa 2012. It is for this reason that there should be great cause for concern when they appear completely incapable of functioning when things do not go according to the plans carefully laid out in their academic texts.

For example, a properly functioning banking

OF MONEY AND METALS: THE OPERATION OF A FREE MONEY SUPPLY EXPLAINED

system would have no problem figuring out what to do with non-performing loans (the common name for the toxic assets that the central bankers so dread). In fact, a properly functioning banking system, where real and not limitless fiduciary money was at stake, would have created an adequate quality control system to ensure that very few financial assets of the toxic variety would live to see the light of day. Those that did see the light of day would have been properly discounted to the point where all of their toxic side effects could be properly cleaned up should they inadvertently spill over.

If we presuppose that a properly functioning banking system would tacitly create internal quality control systems to ensure that the effects of toxic financials assets would be mitigated, and we further suppose that today, a great number of banks and financial institutions are burdened by said toxic financial assets to the point that they must turn to the government and/or central bank as a buyer of last resort, we must assume, then, that there is something dreadfully wrong with the banking system.

What could it be?

As we began to ponder this question, we saw a post by an Ivy League trained economist, who will remain unnamed. His post contained the assertion that fiduciary money is money proper *{Editor's note: Fiduciary money is, in fact, debt that acts and circulates in the place of money}*. This false assertion bothered us to the point where we were compelled to jump in to correct what we assumed to be his unintentional error.

As the reader will see in the interaction that follows, the Ivy league trained economist indulged us for a time and then, for reasons unknown, disabled commenting on the post. We interpret this action as a concession of the point we are trying to make, either that or they just wanted to get rid of us, which, given our obvious charm, we can only assume is not the case.

What is important is that the post brought up a fallacy that we see it as part of our mission here at The Mint to debunk.

The fallacy, which is widely accepted as fact not only by Ivy League trained economists, but also by money managers and central bankers the world over as well, is that fiduciary money operates like money when in reality it is nothing more than a cleverly disguised debt instrument.

So which is it? Is The Mint off his rocker or is there something to the error of this debt-is-money point of view, as in, it may be causing otherwise intelligent people to act in more and more absurd ways as the inevitable consequences of using debt as money continue to rear their ugly head?

Simply stated, is fiduciary money really money, as the name implies, or is it debt? It is a fine point that, to be honest, does not matter to most people on the planet, for what is commonly known as fiduciary money tends to operate as money in a way that is imperceptible to most members of society. In fact, fiduciary money will continue to operate as money...until it doesn't.

For the true essence of fiduciary money is not money at all, but debt. Granted, it may be a highly

OF MONEY AND METALS: THE OPERATION OF A FREE MONEY SUPPLY EXPLAINED

liquid and highly transferable form of debt, but that does not change the fact that when it is created at the bank, be it a local or central bank, it represents a debt of that bank, regardless of the ability of said bank to redeem the fiduciary money for specie money, which is what we hold out as worthy of the term money for purposes of analysis.

As you can see from our presentation of the interaction below, we attempted, in good faith, to convince the Ivy League trained economist that Federal Reserve notes, as their name implies, are debt and not money proper, or specie money.

We have redacted the amicable interaction to highlight the text which is applicable and pertains to the question at hand, is fiduciary money really money?

Please read on and decide for yourself.

*{**Editor's note**: Out of respect for the Ivy League trained economist, we have removed all references to their identity, for it is not our intent to shame, discredit, or launch any form of personal attack on them, but rather to debunk the fallacy surrounding mainstream economics' treatment of fiduciary money in its analysis}.*

Beginning of Transcript:

The Mint (in response to the lengthy initial post which contained the widely held assertion that fiduciary money is money proper, or specie money):

"I would like to point out that fiduciary money is not money, but rather debt which carries in its value a monetary premium which the market has chosen to assign it."

Ivy League trained economist:

"Perhaps this helps you David Mint. I wrote this back on March 8th.

{Link to content further asserting that fiduciary money is money proper, again, the content is removed to protect economist's identity}

The Mint:

"Thanks again, however, I still cannot concede your assertions that Federal Reserve notes are money, rather, they are a debt instrument, which is often referred to as fiduciary money.

The proof of this lies in that Federal Reserve notes pay interest and trade at an implied discount rate, whereas money simply trades against other goods in a varying relationship determined by the relative scarcity of resources.

Both circulate as currency in a normal economy, but the rigidity of debt makes it unsuitable for obligatory legal tender.

It is a fine point that is categorically overlooked, but the more one forces debt into the role of money, the greater the disconnect between the activities of men and the resources available to support those

OF MONEY AND METALS: THE OPERATION OF A FREE MONEY SUPPLY EXPLAINED

activities.

I would love to hear a convincing argument that debt is money if you have one in your archives.

Thanks again and all the best!"

Ivy League trained economist:

"Decidedly David Mint, Federal Reserve notes do not pay interest. There isn't anyone on earth paying interest to anyone else who is holding a $5 bill in his wallet.

Here, David, disabuse yourself. See my many shares on what money is:

{Link to content further asserting that fiduciary money is money, removed to protect economist's identity}

You ought to spend good time reading this one:"

{Link to content further asserting that fiduciary money is money, removed to protect economist's identity}

The Mint

"Quickly, on the fallacy of the $5 bill which is held, the implied interest and discount rate on Federal Reserve notes traded amongst commercial and central banks still affect the value of the bill as it is held up until the moment it is given in exchange for trade. The coupon

rate is 0%, but the normal operations of debt instruments hold true for them.

From what admittedly little I have read of your work, I agree with 99% of what you present. It is this fine point, that Federal Reserve notes behave as debt, even when they are part of the M1 money supply, that I believe is the error which is spread throughout mainstream economics. Of this, I have yet to be disabused by what you have presented.

Debt includes all fiduciary money. The point is important because using debt as money works until it doesn't, meaning the issuer of the debt defaults or is widely perceived to have defaulted, and their debts become worthless in trade."

Ivy League trained economist:

"That's all fine, except Federal Reserve bank notes are not debt. Decidedly, Federal Reserve bank notes are money owning to bearer negotiability and ability to extinguish contracts.

Yet, Federal Reserve notes are not credits, and thus are not debt. Federal Reserve notes are not even evidences of ownership of contracts.

At most anyone can say is that Federal Reserve notes represent a call on future products to be made by anonymous, as yet, identified others who likely shall take them in exchange."

The Mint

OF MONEY AND METALS: THE OPERATION OF A FREE MONEY SUPPLY EXPLAINED

"As a matter of accounting necessity, the Federal Reserve must book a liability when it issues a Federal Reserve Note which makes their notes debt by definition. If this were not the case, why would they list it as a liability on their balance sheet?

*{**Editor's Note:** The Federal Reserve's Balance Sheet, which clearly lists Federal Reserve Notes as liabilities, can be seen at the following hyperlink: http://www.federalreserve.gov/releases/h41/current}*

On the contrary, the most that anyone can say about Federal Reserve notes is that they are the highest and most liquid form of debt that is traded in the US economy. However, this does not change the fact that the essence of the Federal Reserve note is debt."

The Ivy League trained economist unexpectedly exits stage left.

End of Transcript

Who cares? Why is this important? It is important because if what we believe about fiduciary money is true, most of the Western world, including the mysteriously influential Paul Krugman (who is not, by the way, the anonymous Ivy League trained economist in the above transcript), somehow believes that fiduciary money is money proper that can be produced at will, and that the world will be better off if we simply produced more of it.

If the Krugman's of the world get their way, labor and accumulated capital will be so poorly allocated that it could take three generations for humanity to adequately organize itself to make good use of the earth's inexhaustible resources.

Do you have that kind of time?

ARE BITCOINS MONEY? THE CONCEPT OF DIGITAL CURRENCY AND THE DESPERATE NEED FOR A FREE MONEY SUPPLY

*{**Editor's note**: Below is an introduction and redaction of an essay which first appeared on May 9, 2012, addressing the nature of Bitcoins and their fitness, or lack thereof, for use as money proper.}*

So desperate is the world economy for the shackles and inherent limitations of being forced to use debt as money to be removed that they have taken to using any means possible to create the quantities of money necessary for the world economy to operate efficiently. One such currency that has come forward in an attempt to fill the void in the money supply is the Bitcoin. The Bitcoin is a digital currency that has enjoyed an organic type of grassroots growth in popularity. This brief essay examines both the merits and limitations to the

Bitcoin solution in operation today, circa 2013.

Are Bitcoins Money?

We would be remiss here at The Mint if we did not enquire and make an honest attempt to understand the Bitcoin phenomenon. Bitcoins, according to Wikipedia, are units of a peer-to-peer digital currency. They are a purely digital attempt to solve the eternal problem of what to use as money. Are they to be trusted? Let us take a look.

First, we must look at them from a purely conceptual standpoint. Are Bitcoins money? Yes, Bitcoins, as we understand their operation, meet a pure, negative definition of money in the sense that they are not debt.

However, they have a rather severe limitation in that universal or even regional recognition as money in exchange and convertibility to other forms of money could prove elusive. This is a psychological barrier that theoretically could be overcome, however, it is difficult to assume that a majority of persons would, in time, learn what a Bitcoin is and then take the time to sign up for and monitor a Bitcoin wallet, which is the basis for all Bitcoin transactions.

The market penetration for Bitcoins could theoretically be as large as the number of Internet and mobile phone users in the world but would more likely be similar to that of banking customers who use online and mobile banking services. In other words, those who are comfortable storing a portion of their wealth in a digital media.

Given the barriers to recognition and acceptance,

OF MONEY AND METALS: THE OPERATION OF A FREE MONEY SUPPLY EXPLAINED

at this point Bitcoins are probably best thought of as a share of stock in an amorphous payment clearing mechanism whose business model consists of the free exchange of its own shares of stock between account holders and the constant validation of transactions and subsequent logging of ownership of said shares.

These shares, then, would need to be converted into a local currency to be of use in trade outside of the realm of Bitcoin account holders.

The validation of the exchange and the logging of ownership of the Bitcoin stock must be done by someone for the Bitcoins to maintain its integrity and, by extension, any value which others may attach to them apart from a fickle monetary premium which is, at present, compromised by the barriers of recognition and convertibility referred to above.

This validation process is currently undertaken on a voluntarily by the Bitcoin account owners themselves in a process called mining. The act of mining a Bitcoin is accomplished by the users offering their resources, in the form of computer hardware, processing power, and electricity that make the validation process possible, to the greater Bitcoin network for this purpose.

In return for the computer hardware, processing power, and electricity which they dedicate to these processes, the Bitcoin account owner that engages in the act of mining receives a quantity of newly created Bitcoins in exchange for the successful completion of a set quantity of validations, which are essentially bookkeeping and auditing functions. These newly issued Bitcoins serve to dilute the value of the stock of existing Bitcoins.

The term "*mining*" is a fairly accurate description of the way in which Bitcoins come into creation, even though the process more resembles accounting than the traditional strip mining of metal ore.

As of this writing we understand that mining Bitcoins on a small scale is not profitable, which in layman's terms means that the cost of the electricity needed to perform the computer processing involved in mining is greater than the current value of the Bitcoins which would come into existence as a result of the computer processing performed.

This calculation is naturally evaluated in terms of US dollars, as we are not yet aware of a utility company that accepts Bitcoins as payment for electric bills.

It would then follow, were normal market forces operate unhindered, that Bitcoin creation would slow as long as this price relationship exists. We will ignore, for the sake of simplicity, the fact that a great deal of Bitcoin "*mining*" is done via bots which use the electricity and computer processing capacity of unwitting hosts, which makes mining profitable for some at the expense of others, and simply state that Bitcoin creation, on net, is currently a losing proposition.

*{**Editor's Note**: Again, this essay was written on May 9, 2012. By early 2013, the process of mining Bitcoins had become very profitable indeed},*

The fact that the mining of Bitcoins is not profitable should, over time, make the existing Bitcoins more valuable in the future as the stock of Bitcoins will either cease to be diluted or will be diluted at a lower rate. This would

OF MONEY AND METALS: THE OPERATION OF A FREE MONEY SUPPLY EXPLAINED

theoretically cause the value of Bitcoins to increase until it again became profitable to mine them, which in turn would lead to an increased rate of dilution of the Bitcoin stock and lower relative value in exchange, etc.

In this sense, the economics of Bitcoins is similar to that of mining precious metals. Another similarity that the Bitcoin has to precious metals is that theoretically there is a logarithm operating which will ultimately place an absolute limit on the number of Bitcoins that can come into existence. This logarithm theoretically places a mathematical limit to the stock of Bitcoins in the same way that nature places a theoretical limit on the extractable amounts of precious metals that can be used as money.

However, Bitcoins have a distinct disadvantage to precious metals owed to the fact that Bitcoins require constant bookkeeping and auditing to maintain the integrity and therefore value of the Bitcoin as money. Precious metals, on the other hand, do not rely upon administrative functions to maintain their value and rely entirely upon their relative value in trade.

Further, we must assume that the bookkeeping and auditing needed to maintain the integrity of the Bitcoin will increase exponentially as Bitcoin production approaches its logarithmically imposed limit, just as the incentive to perform these functions (mining, as it were) continues to diminish.

Given this inevitable dynamic, it is unclear if the integrity of the system can be maintained once the incentive to maintain the integrity of the system, which is currently supplied by the ability to mine

Bitcoins, is removed.

Having said all of that, it is now time to point out the obvious flaw in the Bitcoin model, the flaw which lands Bitcoins squarely in the realm of equity and makes them unfit for long-term use as money: The threat of competing digital currencies which would surely come into existence if the Bitcoin were to gain widespread popularity and acceptance.

*{**Editor's Note**: Subsequent to the penning of this essay, subsets of the Bitcoin, such as the Litecoin, had already begun to emerge.}*

Even with the digital checks and balances on production which are mathematically built into the Bitcoin model, the Bitcoin, like gold, silver, seashells, and fiat currency, fails to completely solve the happy problem which has no ultimate solution: That the infinite increases in trade due to the increased division of labor in the world will require money and debt markets with the flexibility and dynamism that only a completely free money supply can offer.

Gold and silver may hit physical limits, Bitcoins may be limited by logarithms, and debt based fiat currencies will collapse upon themselves. This is proof that none of them, by virtue of physical and psychological limitations, completely fulfill the role of money for man. In fact, they were never meant to.

The ultimate determination of what will serve as money must be left in the hands of the people who are involved in trade. Left to their own devices, people will solve the problem of what is money with an amazing speed and efficiency that can only be summoned by free individuals acting on their own

OF MONEY AND METALS: THE OPERATION OF A FREE MONEY SUPPLY EXPLAINED

free will.

In other words, the only viable solution to money supply issues is to let those who are engaged in trade decide what is most suited as money at a given time and allow them to trade among themselves without hindrance.

For it is not the costs associated in the production of a monetary unit which remove value from the economy, rather, the administrative burdens, unnecessary conversion costs, and the rigidity of an imposed monetary unit which deals mortal blows to trade and consequently the ability of all humans to flourish to the greatest of their abilities.

Unnatural restrictions on the money supply, which solutions like Bitcoin attempt to solve, are devastating to trade. The destruction wrought by monetary hegemony should surpass hunger, poverty, and climate change as a global concern, for allowing a free money supply to operate would serve to eradicate all of these problems and their symptoms, namely social unrest, terrorism, and health care crises, in a completely organic way that solicits, albeit unwittingly, the tacit cooperation of all involved by virtue of each individual's pursuit of their own self interest.

The ultimate solution to many global problems is within our reach; all that is needed is for the majority to take hold of it. The idea of free money is as simple as it is common to all men for at its base, free money is the purest physical expression of the desire to be free.

THEISM WITH REGARDS TO GOVERNMENT

Anarchy as an Ultimate Given

Volume IV

ATHEISM WITH REGARDS TO GOVERNMENT: ANARCHY AS AN ULTIMATE GIVEN

VOLUME IV

CONTENTS

Introduction: Anarchy as an Ultimate Given	141
Prologue: Portland's Ban on Bisacksuals	144
Dissent is Information: The Primary Reason for the Superiority of Anarchy as a System	147
The Folly of Faith in Government	150
The Kingdom of God is Within You	154
The Test	158
Conclusion	165
Epilogue: Tests in Progress	168
Is America Becoming Ungovernable?	169
Is Atheism with Regards to Government Going Mainstream?	173

INTRODUCTION: ANARCHY AS AN ULTIMATE GIVEN

An·ar·chy -/'anərkē/- noun -1.a: absence of government b: a state of lawlessness or political disorder due to the absence of governmental authority c: a utopian society of individuals who enjoy complete freedom without government 2.a: absence or denial of any authority or established order b: absence of order 3. **atheism with regards to government**

Anarchy. The word strikes fear in the hearts general public, who have been trained to conjure images that range from fraternity house shenanigans to rioting and looting on the streets of important cities at its mere mention. For most civilized persons, with these mental images close at hand, anarchy is something to be avoided at all costs. After all, how can civilized society carry on with the threat of bombs and looting effectively slamming the brakes on human progress?

In this volume, we seek to free the concept of anarchy from these negative connotations. For anarchy, far from being the greater evil in the choice amongst evils when it comes to man's state in this world, is really not a choice at all. Rather, anarchy is something that every human being and animal on the planet is born into. It is the basic state of man in this world. It is an ultimate given.

As an ultimate given, it is futile for men and women to live their lives fretting about the society in which they live falling from a state of order into one of anarchy. This line of thinking is debilitating and counterproductive to what must be seen as mankind's highest and most urgent calling in the physical realm: How best to respond to the state of anarchy in which they live.

For it is not anarchy itself that causes disorder and the various maladies which the mere mention of the word bring to mind, but mankind's failed responses to this ultimate given under which they labor and cause others to labor on their behalf. The only thing more dangerous than confusing anarchy for the disorder which arises from the collapse of a failed response to it is to spend one's life toiling under another person's failed response to his or her inherently anarchic surroundings.

Further, this volume seeks to give the reader a sufficient level of awareness to step back, if even for a moment, and evaluate the response to anarchy under which they are currently laboring and make a sober evaluation as to whether they are truly laboring in alignment with their own best interests.

Too many lives have been wasted laboring under a mistaken fear and avoidance of anarchy, and we

ATHEISM WITH REGARDS TO GOVERNMENT: ANARCHY AS AN ULTIMATE GIVEN

hope this volume will steer the reader away from this fate. It may not change the way you think or what you do at all, and that is good. For to personally validate ones own course in life with a firmer grasp of the facts has caused harm to no one. In fact, it should cause one to carry on with a renewed sense of pride and purpose. If you find yourself in the camp of self-validation, we encourage you to offer others the chance to give their own lives a sober evaluation, and respect as well as encourage their decision to change once they truly understand the wonderful anarchy into which we are all born.

PROLOGUE: PORTLAND'S BAN ON BISACKSUALS

There are certain questions which one encounters in everyday life that demand a shocking answer.

For example, the everyday grocery bagging inquiry *"Would you like paper or plastic?"* can be responded to with one's customary preference of grocery transport. This is the routine response and requires no creativity whatsoever.

A prepared, slightly creative individual may think outside of the box and have their response prepared. *"I don't need a bag, I've brought my own,"* which in today's environmentally conscious age may be interpreted to mean *"I am saving the earth and thereby reject your greedy corporate attempt to deliberately pollute it by rudely offering me an already manufactured bag for my own convenience."*

Then there is the creative genius, the one who rises above the imaginary philosophical bickering and takes what is given to them while at the same time disarming the mythical compulsion which the

ATHEISM WITH REGARDS TO GOVERNMENT: ANARCHY AS AN ULTIMATE GIVEN

slightly creative person above felt threatened by. What is their shocking response to this common question?

"I'll take either one, I'm bisacksual."

In the same way, when approached with the somewhat common question posed by an eager petitioner *"are you registered to vote?"* One can give the standard yes or no answer that the question requires.

The slightly creative person may turn the question into an opportunity to share their point of view. *"That depends, what is the issue?"* Depending upon the issue, they may either wholeheartedly lend their support and sign the petition or engage in a lengthy debate about the error in supporting the proposed legislation.

Enter the creative genius, as in the grocery checkout line, they rise above the imaginary philosophical bickering about what the government should or shouldn't require everyone to do and at the same time disarm the mythical compulsion that caused the slightly creative person to enter into a lengthy and meaningless debate. What, then, is their shocking response to this question?

"I'm an atheist with regards to government."

This volume is dedicated to the creative geniuses.

We currently reside in Portland, Oregon, where plastic bags are frowned upon to the point that the City of Portland passed an ordinance intended to reduce the use of them. The result is that large retailers in Portland are now one-sack outlets, which not only clashes with Portland's tendency towards plurality in any number of spheres, but also has noticeably diminished the overall quality of the paper sacks that are now one's only option at many retailers.

The great irony in the ban on bisacksuality is that the same people seen at City Hall protesting the *"forced"* use of plastic bags are likely to be the same ones who will chain themselves to a tree when the increased demand for paper sacks resulting from this action (the butterfly effect, if you will) leads to the acceleration of the destruction of rainforests in the Amazon.

On the bright side, the plastic bag ban and resulting plea to save the rainforests should combine to help Oregon's ailing lumber industry in the short term.

Yet all of this nonsense about plastic bags, the rejection of bisacksual Portlanders, and the backdoor stimulation of the Oregon lumber industry serves to illustrate the effects that government actions have on both the general population and industry.

The government can hardly be blamed, though. For a government, at its base, is nothing more than the incarnation of the collective response to the anarchy in which we live.

DISSENT IS INFORMATION: THE PRIMARY REASON FOR THE SUPERIORITY OF ANARCHY AS A SYSTEM

Anarchy is the primary state of being for all humans, whether we recognize it or not. The sooner one realizes that they live in a state of Anarchy, the better able they will be to operate within it.

More often than not, mankind collectively seeks to confront and manage these inherently anarchic conditions by employing varying degrees of centralized control mechanisms known as government.

However, centralized control, when exercised without consent, is bad for all involved, both for would be controllers as well as for those being controlled.

Fortunately, anarchic systems have a way of dealing with centralized control by forcing the disbandment of any form of control that is not obtained by assent. Not by assent of the majority, as democratic thought would have us believe, but by the assent of each affected individual. As such, if one is involuntarily subject to a form of centralized control, there is an easy escape for those who are not physically detained. The escape hatch is conveniently located in the mind of each individual, as all centralized control mechanisms can be escaped by changing one's mind about the power the mechanism holds over them.

As both Anarchy and its antithesis, centralized control, coexist to some extent all around us in various forms of ultimately voluntary capitalist and socialist systems which are constantly interacting with each other, it is often difficult, if not impossible, to understand why a state of anarchy can be superior to centralized control.

Charles Hugh-Smith recently wrote an essay on Zerohedge.com entitled, *Why Centralization Leads to Collapse*, which articulates what we believe to be the primary reason the for the superiority of Anarchy as a system (or non-system, as it were):

Dissent is information

Hugh-Smith, in a concise, well-written piece, recognizes that centralized control, which is an natural outgrowth of the desire for efficiency, leads to the rejection and ultimate termination of viewpoints that do not agree with the ideology or methods of the central authority. Under central control, dissent is ignored, hindered, and in extreme cases, terminated.

However, in suppressing dissent, the centralized

authority has removed perhaps the most important means by which a system can transmit vital information from the margins to those who may need to act upon such information.

This marginal information is important, as are the activities that dissenters carry out, for their diverse and seemingly contrary activities serve to make the entire system in which people live "*antifragile*," (to borrow the title of the recent book by Nassim Nicholas Taleb, author of the recent bestseller *The Black Swan*). This means, for practical purposes, that an anarchic system is better prepared to deal with changes in data and the natural environment because it is constantly dealing with it by default, while a centralized system labors under the delusion that's contingency plans are adequate to stave off any event that would threaten the supposedly superior system.

The rejection of dissent, then, ensures the collapse of the centralized system, while the tolerance inherent in an anarchic system ensures its resilience. It may be said that the chief virtue of Anarchy, then, is its prevention of centralized control.

THE FOLLY OF FAITH IN GOVERNMENT

As Henry Hazlitt astutely observed in his classic *Economics in one lesson*, actions taken by central governments have the exact opposite long term effect on reality as that which was intended. For this reason alone, all government mandates must be met with suspicion, regardless of the nobility of their intentions.

Yet none of these government actions and the resulting imbalances would be possible without an unwavering faith in the government on the part of the people, which is why the only hope for the world to escape the crazy cycles inherent in placing faith in the government is for the populace to become not militant, but agnostic towards the actions of their government, as they would a well intentioned but clumsy sidekick.

For government, as we have stated before, is simply the incarnation of a collective response to anarchy. The incarnation will resurrect itself for as

ATHEISM WITH REGARDS TO GOVERNMENT: ANARCHY AS AN ULTIMATE GIVEN

long as the collective seeks a uniform response to the problems presented by living in an inherently anarchic environment. The only way to truly overcome what we classify as failed responses to anarchy, which is what all governments eventually become, is to embrace Anarchy as an ultimate given and learn to operate in it as an individual. Then, and only then, can groups of experienced individuals hope to mount a coherent response to their anarchic surroundings as a collective.

Take the example of Portland's plastic bag ban. Were the disenfranchised bisacksual population of Portland to violently oppose the plastic bag police (which, most certainly, do not exist), they would be wasting their time and resources only to perpetuate a system which promises nothing more but endless power struggles and the short lived thrill of victory or agony of defeat.

Even if bisacksuality were to be again made legal, no sooner would the ink be dry on the new ordinance than would a band of sacktivist warriors covered in plastic armor be organizing to take back their right to a paper only Portland. The bisacksuals would then organize and revolt, and so on.

To be clear, we personally have no strong feelings one way or the other on the sack issue, we have merely chosen to shamelessly embellish upon the theme in order to make a larger point.

The point is that militancy breeds militancy, and violence breeds violence. Constant power struggles are symptoms of the disease of a forced collective response to anarchy.

Champions of non-resistance, such as William Lloyd Garrison in 19th century America, and more recently Gandhi and Martin Luther King, Jr., understood that long term, permanent change could never come about by force of arms. Rather, they understood that the only way to test whether or not an idea was an imperative of natural law or simply a rule born of temporary public opinion was to live in peaceful defiance of the idea and tolerate whatever opposition they met with. If the collective were indeed right, they would eventually encounter natural barriers to impede their actions. If the collective were wrong, it would ultimately employ force to stop them.

In the case of King, the good reverend was thrust into the civil rights battle in the Southern US. For those who may be unfamiliar with this piece of history, we will oversimplify it by saying that there were rules in the South that demanded that African Americans be segregated from White Americans in various aspects of public and private life. Amongst these was a rule that required African American riders to sit towards the back of the public buses.

Rosa Parks and thousands of other African Americans began to put this rule to the test, not by petitioning the powers that be for permission to sit in front of the bus, but rather, by sitting in front of the bus as if the rule did not exist.

Would some supernatural force come and move her to the back of the bus? Or would those who used the rule to gain privilege for themselves be the ones who would force her to the back of the bus or even deny her entry onto the bus in the first place?

The creative geniuses amongst us already know the answer.

The deeper question that must be addressed,

ATHEISM WITH REGARDS TO GOVERNMENT: ANARCHY AS AN ULTIMATE GIVEN

then, is not whether or not each individual rule is necessary, but rather, is a government that imposes rules and forces those affected to comply with those rules a necessity? Or is it merely an imaginary framework used to erect a series of rules that are imposed by one group on other groups in order to gain or maintain an unearned privilege?

The only valid way to test this theory would be for one to live their life as if the government did not really exist. What if one were to test this theory not by withdrawing from the government or fighting to change it, for both courses of action would be to acknowledge its existence, but by simply deciding not to believe in the government? What if one decided to stop attributing power to the government by simply changing their own mind about its existence and acting accordingly?

In other words, what if the simplest path to freedom were to become an atheist with regards to government?

THE KINGDOM OF GOD IS WITHIN YOU

"I am an atheist with regards to the world's governments, for I have chosen to live in the Kingdom of God"

A ride through Portland's plastic bag ban, bisacksuality, the virtues of non-violent protest, Anarchy, atheism, and the imaginary construct of government has lead us to an uncomfortable confrontation with our inner anarchist. Isn't Anarchy a bad thing? Aren't anarchists generally bad people, who wish destruction and chaos in place of the order that we now enjoy?

In the previous chapter, we have proposed that the best way to test the legitimacy of government, that is, its right to govern, would be to simply live as if the government did not exist and see where resistance came from.

If resistance were to come from a majority of individuals who are directly affected by one's

ATHEISM WITH REGARDS TO GOVERNMENT: ANARCHY AS AN ULTIMATE GIVEN

actions, then that would lend credence to the necessity and legitimacy of government. If, however, resistance were to appear in the form of a minority relying on an imaginary framework to create and enforce a series of rules that are imposed by one group on other groups in order to gain or maintain an unearned privilege, the legitimacy of the government must be called into question.

For if the government does not work to assist people in working together to form adequate responses to their naturally anarchic state, it is hindering them. There is no neutrality when it comes to claiming a sovereign right over individuals. The claim of this sovereign right implies, by default, that the sovereign entity, in our example the government, will have an impact on the actions of the individual. If this is not the case, the sovereign right is nothing more than an illusion.

Not that it is necessarily the legitimacy of those who are governing at the time that would be questioned, although it is implied, but rather the legitimacy of the apparatus which allows such rule by the minority at the expense of the majority. If a majority would be materially better off by simply shedding the illusion of government, why does the idea of government persist as a seemingly permanent part of the collective conscience?

To briefly answer this question, for it demands a response, the idea of government and its companion, central banking, have risen as mans' collective response to help him deal with his anarchic surroundings. As the idea of government seems to address what would be man's chief preoccupations, were he to acknowledge that he stands naked before the anarchic forces around him, it is natural that this idea would be ingrained in the man's psyche to such an extent that it would drive not only a majority of his own decisions, but also those of his descendants.

Let's face it; it is nice to sleep at night with the idea that someone is watching over us and our assets. Even more comfort may be had in the idea that, were something to happen to us or our assets, we would still be taken care of.

Yet given the inherent uncertainty, what we now know as Anarchy, in which we all are obliged to operate, most thinking humans would only dare ascribe the ability to provide universal care to an omniscient and omnipotent deity. Why, then, would it make sense to attribute the power of an all-powerful and all seeing deity to what generally amounts to an assembly of fallible men?

Ever since Adam and Eve were kicked out of the Garden of Eden, men and women have confronted a world that is in a state of anarchy. Given that anarchy demands a response, men and women tend to quickly submit to whatever promises them protection from these anarchic forces. Once they have made the choice to submit, it is extremely difficult to change paths. These yokes to which persons willing submit are commonly known as religion and patriotism. However, if one recognizes that there is an opportunity to change paths, as those who have arrived at this point in this volume most likely have by now, the implications are staggering.

Is it indeed possible to be an atheist with regards to the world's governments? Is it possible to not toil

ATHEISM WITH REGARDS TO GOVERNMENT: ANARCHY AS AN ULTIMATE GIVEN

for or against them, but simply to view life as an exercise in dealing with the inconveniences which appear as a result of a large part of the world's population acting upon the belief that the government really exists?

To paraphrase Paul in the Biblical book of Romans, is it possible to live in the world but not be of the world by merely transforming one's way of thinking? For this is the essence of living in the Kingdom of God. As Tolstoy chose to title his magnum opus, so we submit to those who are able to accept it: *The Kingdom of God is within you*.

The only way to know whether or not this staggering choice truly exists is to peacefully and actively test the hypothesis of a government's legitimacy. How can these tests be performed?

THE TEST

In the previous chapter, we presented a hypothesis for dealing with the world's governments. Namely, living as if the government does not exist and seeing where the resistance, if any, comes from. Now, we must move the hypothesis down a level. How, then would one test the hypothesis by embracing Anarchy, or atheism with regards to government, in a place like Oregon?

Oregon is a State that places a relatively large amount of faith in its political system and, by extension, the power of the government to solve social problems.

The approach seems to work for most. The territory is home to an abundance of natural resources and a great number of people who are willing to go along with the government's program. In these conditions, the idea and mechanisms of government are tolerated and to an extent championed, for it is possible to live in Oregon and enjoy a relatively high standard of living despite the

ATHEISM WITH REGARDS TO GOVERNMENT: ANARCHY AS AN ULTIMATE GIVEN

waste inherent in governmental activities.

However, one can only wonder as to what might be here in the great Northwest were the government not to hyper regulate every industry or confiscate 9% of the wages earned by its laborers on top of the roughly 21% that the Federal government lays claim to.

Is the average citizen better off living on just 70% of their wages? Or, put another way, does the average citizen derive enough benefit from being governed that he or she would value it at roughly one third of his or her income?

There are burning questions that every citizen would do well to ask of themselves, if not their government, from time to time. If the mechanism of government were to go away, or be reduced to the spheres where it paradoxically does add value to the economy (note that, were this the case, it would technically cease to be government, per se, and become yet another enterprise operating in the inherently anarchic surroundings), would it not hold that everyone, including those who work in the unproductive areas of government, would be better off on a relative basis?

The answer, of course, is yes, unless one finds themselves in a position which relies upon the government being able to confiscate a certain amount of resources on their behalf in order to support their livelihood, or finds themselves employed by an enterprise that can only continue to operate with the protection of certain privileges which the mechanism of government may grant them.

However, even this minority would be better off

once they adjusted to the reality of life without the idea of government.

What about the Disaster aid, Police and Fire Departments? Aren't they at least indispensible functions of the government?

Of course they are! And for that very reason, private organizations would quickly spring up to replace the government agencies that currently perform these vital roles in society. In fact, they already exist. They are commonly known as Security and Insurance companies. In Anarcho-Capitalist thought, the companies that would arise are called Private Defense Agencies. Anyone skeptical about what would naturally arise in a purely anarchic system to replace functions currently delegated to the State is encouraged to study this theory.

Yet despite the alternatives, the mechanism of the state remains in place and retains a monopolistic power over defense, income redistribution in the form of taxes, as well as the right to generally meddle in all of the affairs of its subjects in the name of promoting security and equality.

As with any failing entity, when a government has gone from being a servant of the people to active enslavement of the populace, its lack of popularity will tend to manifest itself in its own deteriorating financial condition. This fact alone is proof that Anarchy is the context in which the Nation States of the world act and operate. In the final analysis, the world's governments are subject to the same immutable economic laws that individuals and collectives are. On this basis alone it is proper to constantly question the relevancy of the State with regards to its utility against viable alternatives, for both nation states and individuals are equally subject to the forces of natural law.

Next, we will examine the condition of a failing nation-state. It has been observed throughout history that the authorities of a failing nation state or other similar group which has taken for itself a monopoly on defense, rarely give up their arms willingly or peacefully, so it is up to the individual to peacefully disarm it.

For disarming it is the only way that mankind can return to square one and bravely face the anarchy in which we live. Once we soberly face our anarchic surroundings, it will be clear what is to be done by all, and the tacit communication amongst individuals, commonly referred to as the market, can begin to quickly and efficiently help us to solve our common problems.

How can one go about peacefully disarming an entity that has unilaterally claimed the privilege of maintaining armaments and effective control of other functions which, based on economic imperatives, must necessarily be left to individuals? For practical purposes, we have compiled a brief list of steps that one could take to peacefully resist a non-aggressive nation state that is at peace from within. Each step proposed is a step away from what on the surface appear to be unnecessary rules, and a step towards effectively solving the problems that are a result of our anarchic surroundings:

1. **Money, Trade what you want to:** Conduct trade in a currency other than the one used to pay the tax. For it is proper to give to Caesar what is Caesar's, and at the same time, there is no

supernatural obligation to use Caesar's money. Render tax declarations only on the amount of trade conducted using the imperial coin and currency.

2. **Rely on Common sense**: Ignore laws and other excessive regulations in favor of respect for the free will of those you hire. If someone is willing to work for you for less than minimum wage, allow them to work, do not deprive them of a job to comply with an arbitrary wage rate set by a bureaucrat. Make no conscious distinction between contract workers and employees, for both are performing work, regardless of arbitrary external distinctions implied by laws and regulations.

3. **An important caveat** to this is to not brag about flouting unreasonable laws and regulations. Assume that if you are breaking a legitimate law, both you and the employee will know of it and have dealt with it long before the government will deal with it. It is the false hope that government is regulating untenable working conditions that gives rise to untenable working conditions in the first place.

4. **Come out of Babylon:** If you live in a place where the microscope of government regulation is unavoidable and unbearable, physically relocate until you have created a safe distance between the regulations and your livelihood.

5. **Cross borders:** If language is not a barrier and your trade or profession is not location specific, there should be no resistance from either

ATHEISM WITH REGARDS TO GOVERNMENT: ANARCHY AS AN ULTIMATE GIVEN

government to crossing national borders in search of better opportunities, for all stand to benefit from this.

6. **Sell what consumers want**, not what the government allows you to sell. The greatest test of a product (food included) is public opinion. Government approval of products, like labor laws tend to give the population a false sense of security.

As we have stated above, if the nation state in which one lives operates with intentions that are pure and in harmony with natural law, they should offer no resistance to an individual who chooses to take these steps. Any resistance will come from voluntary actions taken by the individuals who are directly affected, and the natural consequences of failing to do the right thing will fall squarely on one's own shoulders.

If, on the other hand, the nation state begins to pass and enforce laws against these actions, it will have shown itself to be predatory. Far from existing to help people deal with their anarchic surroundings, it will be hindering them from doing so.

Anyone who has attempted to take the steps above has likely encountered some sort of resistance to taking these actions. What may come as a surprise is that the resistance may not have come directly from the government itself, but from disinterested yet well-meaning citizens who have tried to deter these brave souls on the basis of blind obedience to the rules.

What these well-intentioned citizens fail to

realize is that blind obedience to the rules makes slaves of everyone.

CONCLUSION

Anarchy is an ultimate given. The rise of the current system of nation states is simply the latest rendition of an attempt by man to bring order to chaos. This latest attempt, like every other attempt at maintaining a far-reaching empire since the dawn of time, is flawed.

For no man or group of men, regardless of their number, clairvoyance, or special powers they profess to have, can suspend or accelerate the operation of natural law. The Creator alone reserves that power for himself.

Viewed from above, nation states are not ultimate givens, and therefore are incapable of spawning natural laws of their own accord. The best they can do is to assist individuals in their common toil to comply with the demands of the state of anarchy in which they live. However, most versions of the nation state, circa 2013, are working on a large-scale basis to at best delay and at worst suppress the ability of the individual to respond to the demands of the natural laws to which we are all subject.

Nation states are merely the prevailing defense agencies in their geographical region that initially lay claim to the allegiance and a portion of the output of those who are born within their borders. The proof of this fact is in the following: It is true that if one comes to the point of disenchantment with their current nation state, it is possible, yet expensive and perhaps dangerous, to choose amongst which nation state one will submit to. In this sense, nation states can be said to be collective entities that have seized the right to guide a person's response to anarchy at birth. Another proof lies in the manner in which nation states negotiate amongst themselves and with corporations.

Given this understanding of the nation state, it would follow that revolutions are simply extreme reactions to poor customer service, and not a valid claim to a moral high ground as many revolutionaries throughout the ages have professed. When one has a complaint with the way they are being served, the normal response is to take one's business elsewhere, not make an attempt to become CEO of the entity by which they have been treated badly.

We pray that this volume has helped to shatter any preconceived notions regarding Anarchy. For Anarchy is not a boogeyman, rather, it is atheism with regards to government. As such, a state of anarchy does not imply that rules and regulations, which are indispensable for humans to live together in harmony and to plan their daily activities, should be banished.

ATHEISM WITH REGARDS TO GOVERNMENT: ANARCHY AS AN ULTIMATE GIVEN

Anarchy is an ultimate given, and the state of anarchy is constantly in demand of an active response. Due to the urgency felt by all of mankind to respond to the state of anarchy, there will always be rules and regulations. However, a proper understanding of Anarchy as an ultimate given means that persons, instead of being under compulsion to submit to rules and regulations, will voluntarily consent to live by such rules and regulations within a territory or within a certain social sphere because the rules provide an undeniable benefits that all adherents are free to partake in.

While a common response to mankind's inherently anarchic state is always beneficial, an understanding of and appeal to Anarchy, and not allegiance to a corporation or nation state, allows the greater part of mankind to both tacitly and expressly form appropriate responses to anarchy in the present. It will allow lessons learned to disseminate faster and assist more in their chosen response to anarchy than ever before.

For Anarchy is not something to be feared, it is the very essence of freedom.

EPILOGUE: TESTS IN PROGRESS

After reflecting on the ideas which we have presented in this volume, we began to look for evidence of people putting their faith in government to the ultimate test. What we found shocked us. The phenomenon, far from being on the fringe, is already underway in America and throughout much of the world. The following posts, which first appeared on The Mint on August 11, 2011 and July 12, 2012, respectively, explore this interesting phenomenon.

IS AMERICA BECOMING UNGOVERNABLE?

{***Editor's Note***: *This essay first appeared on* The Mint *on August 17, 2011}*

August thoughts in the US are being rudely interrupted by the presidential campaigns that are warming up in Iowa and are heading to New Hampshire to continue the race in which the winner will declare themselves King of the Americans.

As Bloom County fans may recall, when the Meadow party nominated Bill the Cat and Opus for President and Vice President in 1984, they concluded that only a complete idiot would apply after careful consideration of the job description which, in their estimation, included *"being blamed for every problem on the planet."*

The complete idiot label came to mind after we heard a comment in a video shared with us by a friend in which Bill Hybels, the Pastor of Willow

Creek, a large church in Illinois, noted that the tendency in American dialogue today is to "*throw stones first and ask questions later.*" He explained that people grab onto comments and statements made by others and publicly villianize them without bothering to consider the context or verify the validity of said statements.

His remarks were made at the Willow Global Leadership Summit while addressing the interesting situation in which Howard Schultz, the CEO of Starbucks, backed out of his contract to appear at the summit after receiving threats of a boycott from a group who claimed that Willow Creek was against homosexuals.

Mr. Hybels went on to say that this phenomenon is making America ungovernable.

He did not go into detail as to how the "*throw stones first, ask questions later,*" phenomenon would make the country ungovernable, but the idea got us thinking all the same. What makes a country governable in the first place? Do people naturally need government in order to survive?

In the sense that people need to feel protected and able to care for themselves and their loved ones, people may, at a minimum, need to believe in the concept of government. People, knowing their weak state on this planet, need to believe that someone is looking out for them. This need leads them to subject themselves to the idea of government.

Inevitably, those who are entrusted with embodying the idea of government find that they are given quite a bit of power over the lives of others and quickly learn to abuse it.

This leads the subjects to seek freedom from the

ATHEISM WITH REGARDS TO GOVERNMENT: ANARCHY AS AN ULTIMATE GIVEN

government while at the same time looking for someone or something else to fulfill their basic need for physical protection and material well being. Seen this way, when a people become ungovernable, they are rejecting the government that they find themselves subject to because of perceived or actual abuses by or the impotence of the government with regards to fulfilling their needs.

It is important to note that, for people to reach this state, they must feel that they are out of options under their current government. Economic hardship has a lot to do with how people perceive their options, and it should come as no surprise that the level of economic hardship has a positive correlation to the number and reach of laws and policies enacted by governments to restrict the freedoms of individuals.

Free men are infinitely more productive than slaves. And policy changes in either direction will express itself in economic results. Are the people freer or more enslaved as a collective result of the policies in place? The recent economic data coming out of the United States of America prove that we are a people becoming enslaved.

When things go well, no one cares who is governing. When things go badly, they become unnaturally preoccupied with the political process. America, circa 2011, is moving dangerously towards this unnatural preoccupation.

Ironically, the more one concentrates on the government and its political processes, the more it becomes evident that the very existence of a government organized by men may be more of a threat to than a protector of the basic needs of protection and material well-being that have given rise to the concept of government in the first place.

In practice, the governments of the world today operate like competing defense agencies. It may be, then, that Americans are tired of the current contractor and are searching for another one; one that is less intrusive and has fewer overhead costs to cover.

Will they find it before they are completely enslaved by the current one?

IS ATHEISM WITH REGARDS TO GOVERNMENT GOING MAINSTREAM?

*{**Editor's Note**: This essay first appeared on The Mint on July 12, 2012}*

We recently subscribed to Gary North's latest project, a site called "*The Tea Party Economist*." To be clear, we have no political interest nor affiliation, period. It is our feeling that government, in its current state, is best ignored and avoided rather than confronted. If ignored, it will eventually go away, one way or another. While we may have no confidence or belief in government, we make up for it in an abundance of faith in God and our fellow men and women.

To draw on a well known analogy, in our view the Tea Party, together with the Republican and Democratic parties, are fighting for control of the steering wheel of the Titanic after it hit the iceberg. Rather than fight it out on the control deck, we at The Mint realize that the only ones who survived the

Titanic were those who found a lifeboat or other means to stay afloat.

Today, Mr. North shared an article on the site which made us gasp. It was written by Jerry Bowyer and, as we read through it, one thought repeatedly passed through our mind:

"Has our manner of thinking really gone mainstream?"

Mr. Bowyer points out a number of examples of a general decline in voluntary compliance with things that the government increasingly uses its superior force to mandate, such as taxes and environmental laws. The irony is that as a government's power grab via rules and regulations accelerates, voluntary compliance, from which all forms of government ultimately derive their power, declines. It is clear, yet seldom acknowledged, that the absence of voluntary compliance is the most effective type of revolution which can be waged.

If Mr. Bowyer is correct, then it would appear that Americans are taking the idea of atheism with regards to government to heart.

Mr. Bowyer also makes an important distinction which we wish to highlight, for it is very important. The lack of voluntary compliance is not a form of civil disobedience or act of aggression towards a government. Rather, it is the conscious choice to stop believing in the government and live one's life as if it does not exist as anything more than a lethal nuisance to be avoided. Mr. Bowyer eloquently describes this phenomenon via an amoeba metaphor:

ATHEISM WITH REGARDS TO GOVERNMENT: ANARCHY AS AN ULTIMATE GIVEN

"It's not civil disobedience that I'm talking about. It's the opposite: Civil disobedience is meant to be noticed. It is a price paid in the hope of creating social change. What I'm talking about is not based on hope; in fact, it has given up much hope on social change. It thinks the government is a colossal amoeba twitching mindlessly in response to tiny pinpricks of pain from an endless army of micro-brained interest groups. The point is not to teach the amoeba nor to guide it, but simply to stay away from the lethal stupidity of its pseudopods."

"The amoeba does not get smarter but it does get hungrier and bigger. On the other hand, we get smarter. More and more of our life takes place outside of the amoeba's reach: in the privacy of our own homes, or in capital accounts in other nations, or in the fastest growing amoeba avoidance zone ever created, cyberspace. We revolt decision by decision, transaction by transaction, because we believe deep down that most of what government tells us to do is at bottom illegitimate."

*{**Editor's Note**: You can read the entire article here at Forbes.com: July 4th Question, Part III: Americans Revolt Billions of Times a Day}*

Everyday, more and more people are recognizing the insanity of attempting to comply with the onslaught of rules and regulations which allegedly protect them against others. They are realizing that the rules are building a prison in which they themselves are incarcerated.

We conclude these thoughts with a quote from Ayn Rand's novel *Atlas Shrugged*, which seems most appropriate when considering an amoeba-like government:

"When you see that trading is done, not by consent, but by compulsion – when you see that in order to produce, you need to obtain permission from men who produce nothing – when you see that money is flowing to those who deal, not in goods, but in favors – when you see that men get richer by graft and by pull than by work, and your laws don't protect you against them, but protect them against you – when you see corruption being rewarded and honesty becoming a self-sacrifice – you may know that your society is doomed."

Natural Law and the Theory of Economic System Fluidity

Marx and Rand together in perfect harmony

Volume V

NATURAL LAW AND THE THEORY OF ECONOMIC SYSTEM FLUIDITY: MARX AND RAND TOGETHER IN PERFECT HARMONY

VOLUME V

CONTENTS

Nature's Struggle: An Introduction	180
A Tale of Two Responses to Anarchy	185
SECTION I - TRUE CAPITALISM	187
The Tenets and Benefits of True Capitalism	187
True Capitalism as Natural Law	192
True Capitalism: Superior to and Incompatible with the Nation State	194
The Nation State's Campaign Against True Capitalism	198
True Capitalism vs. Might Makes Right	201
The Characteristics of a Truly Capitalistic Society	204
SECTION II - NATURAL LAW	207

Natural Law: The Transcendental Importance of Supply, Demand, and Equilibrium Prices	207
The Golden Rule	214
An Example of the Operation of the Golden Rule	218
The Question of Charity	221
True Capitalism Enables Compliance with the Golden Rule	223
The Theory of Economic System Fluidity: Marx and Rand Together in Perfect Harmony	225
Conclusion	233

NATURE'S STRUGGLE: AN INTRODUCTION

The natural world strives daily to achieve a perfect state of balance. Events and occurrences that, taken by themselves, appear chaotic and devoid of meaning are together part of a constant rebalancing of the earth's delicate state. Each event is a splash of color across an oppressive gray sky that hints at a rainbow that will soon appear.

The natural world exists in a constant state of subtle agitation and violent quakes, yet each and every ebb and flow in the natural world is the physical expression of its desire to achieve a state that by definition will never be perfected:

Homeostasis.

Homeostasis, the tendency toward a relatively stable equilibrium between interdependent elements, is a state of being that all at once already exists and ultimately will never exist, for the natural

NATURAL LAW AND THE THEORY OF ECONOMIC SYSTEM FLUIDITY: MARX AND RAND TOGETHER IN PERFECT HARMONY

world's constant striving towards this state ensures that a perfect balance can never be achieved.

Yet despite the seemingly constant struggles in the natural world, it is ultimately obedient to a firm set of rules. The clashes between immovable objects and irresistible forces, the interplay between predator and prey, and the aggregation of slow processes which unite to cause large scale natural spectacles and events, are themselves the living proof of the immutable natural laws that they are governed by.

Mankind, for all of its virtues, has tacitly adopted a large-scale delusion with regards to the natural world. The delusion is this; that all of nature's struggles, interplays, and slow processes can be tamed or manipulated to bring about a constant state of balance in which he can plan, build, and operate with a high degree of certainty.

The widespread belief in this delusion, while seemingly noble and painstakingly practical, has flourished and proliferated under the current monetary system, in which the monetary premium, the highest expression of value that can be attributed to a good, has been completely removed from the natural world and is largely attributed to debt instruments, which ultimately rest on nothing more than the well intended promises of men.

Mankind's day-to-day activities, which are the result of the choices that each man or woman individually make, often unconsciously, are largely dedicated to obtaining control of a greater portion of the monetary premium. If this is true, it would hold that the activities of mankind, to the extent that they succeed in their pursuit of the monetary premium, serve to throw the natural world ever further out of its delicate balance, which in turn gives rise to nature's need to rebalance itself in order to comply with the incessant demands of natural law.

This volume, which in many ways forms the ideological core of this treatise, deals with natural law and mankind's most suitable response to its many and varied demands, the capitalistic system.

It does so by presenting the tenets and benefits of the true capitalistic system, a system rooted in the principles of freedom and private property. It further examines the specific demands of natural law and mankind's failed response to it, which is the large-scale socialist system that has been violently forced upon mankind through the mechanism of large-scale government. The ideology behind this modern large-scale socialist system is referred to throughout this volume as the might makes right mentality.

Near the end of this volume, we present the Theory of Economic System Fluidity as the basis for understanding the tendency of mankind to pursue socialist ideals on a small scale while competing in the truly capitalistic system on a larger scale. The theory provides a coherent understanding of how economic harmony may be achieved in a world that on the surface appears to be gravitating towards the painful consequences of the ideological polarization demanded by strict adherence to either the virtues of capitalism or the socialist ideal.

The present day predominance of a large-scale socialist system has made possible the current monetary experiment in which central bank debt obligations have garnered an inordinate share of the monetary premium over the past forty years.

While mankind is a mere forty years into the present monetary experiment, the effects of the removal of the monetary premium from the natural world are already evident, and the staggering consequences are manifesting themselves in the natural world through a phenomenon that has taken on the label of climate change.

This label is woefully misleading, as the climate is not simply changing, rather, the whole of the natural world is becoming increasingly unstable as it desperately seeks to balance the activities of men, which previously worked in relative harmony with nature, with the immutable demands of natural law.

The current debt based monetary system and its tendency towards centralized planning and decision making has not only caused significant imbalances in trade and resource allocation, it is increasingly causing the earth itself to react more and more violently as it alone strives to comply with the demands of natural law. For mankind, once the earth's unwitting yet faithful custodian has become its well-meaning adversary.

The root of this growing antagonism between man and nature is the forced misallocation of the monetary premium, and the only remedy is to return the monetary premium to its rightful place in the natural realm. For so long as it rests solely on central bank debt instruments and digitally created currencies, the power of the monetary premium is in the employ of the most destructive force on the planet, the uninhibited hopes and dreams of mankind.

A TALE OF TWO RESPONSES TO ANARCHY

In the current economic debate that rages between the productive virtues of what is referred to as capitalism and the humanistic virtues of the socialist ideal, it has become fashionable to assume that the virtues of one system, were its guiding principles put into action at once by all of the members of society, would eventually bring about the virtues promised by the other system in a peaceful manner.

This narrow, apologetic view taken by capitalists and socialists alike ignores the fact that the systems are wholly incompatible. It also ignores the fact that mankind is in a constant struggle to bring order to surroundings that are inherently anarchic in nature. The only laws that must be adhered to are natural laws, which are explored in section II of this volume.

For purists on either side of the ideological fence, compromise on any point is a slippery slope, and in the sense that the two systems are wholly incompatible, this extreme view is technically correct. However, most economists miss the fact that it is perfectly normal and beneficial for each system to operate side by side. In fact, it is the only way in which mankind can reap the benefits of both systems at once.

All humans live and operate in both systems to some extent. The capitalist system is best equipped to organize resources on a grand scale and provide material goods for the greatest number of people, while the socialist system offers a refuge from the rigid and unrelenting demands of the capitalist system's incessant responses to anarchy and the demands of natural law. This refuge is commonly referred to as the family, and it can be observed operating the world over in all shapes and sizes.

The inescapable fact that capitalism and socialism are at once incompatible and completely reliant upon one another is the basis for the Theory of Economic System Fluidity.

SECTION I - TRUE CAPITALISM

THE TENETS AND BENEFITS OF TRUE CAPITALISM

The Theory of Economic System Fluidity cannot be understood in a vacuum. Nor can it be understood as a unified appeal to natural law. It must be approached in a piecemeal fashion through an exploration of its lesser-understood components, namely, true capitalism and natural law.

In what on the surface may appear yet a further paradox, it is necessary to begin this volume not with an explanation of natural law, as logic may suggest, but with an exploration of the basis of the truly capitalistic system.

For the capitalist system, in its purist form, is a relentless attempt to bring the activities of mankind into compliance with the incessant and ever changing demands of natural law. It is in no way an overstatement to declare that the capitalist system is an expression of mankind's most adequate response to nature's demands. If anything, it is a gross understatement of the system's importance.

While most persons in the economic discipline readily grasp the concept of capitalism, the concept of natural law is elusive to the average economist. Its precepts are entwined with philosophy, metaphysics and many other disciplines that, like the charge of racketeering, cover a lot of ground. As this volume deals with natural law from a primarily economic perspective, the shortest path to understanding natural law for the economist (and most laymen) is through the very lens of capitalism itself.

However, the capitalist system, as the label is understood today, is at best an incomplete and at worst a severely distorted expression of true capitalism. The term true capitalism is used in this volume to clearly differentiate the current day capitalistic system, which embraces many characteristics of socialism, from the truly capitalistic system that consists of mankind's most effective response to the demands of natural law.

What is True Capitalism?

True Capitalism is man's most perfect expression of democracy

True Capitalism enables Justice

True Capitalism enables equality

True Capitalism enables widespread prosperity

NATURAL LAW AND THE THEORY OF ECONOMIC SYSTEM FLUIDITY: MARX AND RAND TOGETHER IN PERFECT HARMONY

True Capitalism is born in and comfortable with Anarchy

True Capitalism requires a radical trust in others

When people refer to a breakdown of society, what they are often referring to is a general breakdown of trust. If there is to be hope for the future, mankind must collectively learn to trust each other again. True Capitalism is a constant test of trustworthiness, and a betrayal of trust is quickly and harshly dealt with within its confines. Conversely, those who are found trustworthy stand to be richly rewarded in a truly capitalistic system. The system's meting out of natural rewards and consequences serves to encourage and consequently increase general trustworthiness.

It then follows that True Capitalism works to improve society by carrying out the natural consequences of actions in a rapid and impartial manner. It encourages men and women to serve one another as they find that serving one another is in their mutual interest. In fact, it is in their rightly understood self-interest (to quote Ludwig Von Mises) to serve one another.

What are the Tenets of True Capitalism?

True Capitalism is a radical respect for both life and private property. It is the recognition that the right of an individual to life and private property are inviolate and that individuals, assured that their life and property are not endangered, will reap the fullest benefits of the division of labor and mutual cooperation which men and women on this earth are capable of.

Participation in the truly capitalistic system is not voluntary, for True Capitalism is not an idealistic concept, rather, it is an ultimate given (for this reason, socialism is not an alternative to True Capitalism, rather, it operates as a subsystem within the framework of True Capitalism). Apart from participation, however, all other actions and agreements that do not violate another's right to life or rightly acquired private property are completely voluntary.

Apart from being a part of the system, nothing done in the truly capitalistic system is obligatory. This is where True Capitalism differs from the system that has come to bear the label "crony capitalism," the system in which most of the world currently operates which is full of random taxes, fees, regulations, and laws which require compulsion or coercion by a nation state in order to ensure compliance.

In the truly capitalistic system, actions such as paying an entity or observing a regulation may be strongly advisable to the point of being considered a necessity, but even these highly advisable actions are not taken under compulsion or the threat of violence by a nation state or another actor in the system.

In a truly capitalistic system, the best way to get ahead (obtain more opportunities, leisure, or whatever else one desires to pursue) is to make oneself useful to his or her fellow man or woman.

NATURAL LAW AND THE THEORY OF ECONOMIC SYSTEM FLUIDITY: MARX AND RAND TOGETHER IN PERFECT HARMONY

The nature of the system is to reward those that best serve others. Those rewarded then find themselves able to consume goods and services freely produced by their fellow man by using the resources they have obtained by doing the same.

Voluntary adherence to the demands of the truly capitalistic system creates a virtuous feedback loop where he or she that is the greatest will be the servant of all.

TRUE CAPITALISM AS NATURAL LAW

If one lifts the veil of the machinations of today's nation state to expose the inherent anarchy in which the nation states of the world operate, it is clear that True Capitalism is more than an ideal, it is part of the operation of the very natural laws to which adherence to the system enables mankind to adapt and react to.

Far from being radical ideas which float around on the fringe of public discourse, True Capitalism and by extension, Anarchy, are ultimate givens within which the current system of nation states are forced to operate. Upon further examination of these facts, it becomes clear that the nation states of the world have largely embraced an ideology that is best described as "might makes right," a system where the most expedient way to get ahead is by resorting to violence to force submission to one's will.

The resulting arms race that is the logical outcome of adherence to the might makes right ideology is the antithesis of the striving to better serve one another which is the measure of success in the truly capitalistic system. The negative side effects of resorting to the extreme actions ultimately demanded by adherence to the might makes right ideology such as genocide and widespread famines are politely explained away by their apologists as "survival of the fittest."

Despite its shortcomings, is not submission to the nation-state a preferable state of being to that of mankind collectively facing their anarchic surroundings without the benefit of the nation state's protection? It is true that if the nation state were to immediately disband, anarchy would reign in its place. However, this condition will not persist, as an anarchic state demands an almost immediate collective response.

Unfortunately, many individuals believe that anarchy would lead to perpetual chaos. However, quite the opposite is true. For out of anarchy, the truly capitalistic system would organically emerge, and with it a new dawn for humanity, built on mutual interest and almost endless capital formation which will engender a spontaneous and dynamic social order; a society without borders that would enjoy freedom and prosperity that mankind cannot even imagine under current conditions.

TRUE CAPITALISM: SUPERIOR TO AND INCOMPATIBLE WITH THE NATION STATE

One's ability to act and react to the rapid changes in the current political and social structures, circa 2013, depends upon accepting and embracing True Capitalism as the basis for reality and learning to operate in the truly capitalistic system which organically emerges as mankind learns that mutual trust and cooperation are in its rightly understood self interests, and that he who is to lead must truly become the servant of all.

To truly embrace True Capitalism, it is necessary to understand something about the nature of mankind. First and foremost, man, left to his own devices, is completely devoid of the ability to do the right thing. He doesn't have it in him. He is lazy, self-serving, and completely evil. He needs God and the encouragement of his fellow man to be able to do anything productive, altruistic, or remotely good.

NATURAL LAW AND THE THEORY OF ECONOMIC SYSTEM FLUIDITY: MARX AND RAND TOGETHER IN PERFECT HARMONY

A full defense of this assertion is beyond the scope of this volume. It is sufficient to state that the evidence of man's moral decay is on display daily in the world's periodicals, if not in one's personal experience. It is mentioned here only to underscore the need for a framework within which mankind can avoid both self and mutual destruction.

There is only one reliable framework that has emerged to address the inherent problem of human nature and at the same time turn mankind's weaknesses into its strengths. This framework is True Capitalism. By allowing market forces to work with as little hindrance as possible, mankind can insulate itself from descending into chaos and catastrophe.

The previous chapter concluded with the following bold declaration:

"The truly capitalistic system would organically emerge, and with it a new dawn for humanity, built on mutual interest and almost endless capital formation which will engender a spontaneous and dynamic social order, and a society without borders that would enjoy freedom and prosperity that we cannot even imagine under current conditions."

The greatest virtue of True Capitalism is the speed with which it corrects human errors in judgment. Bad ideas, malinvestment, fraud, even violent and property crime are often quickly dealt with within its framework.

Why? The reason that True Capitalism is able to quickly jettison mankind's less desirable tendencies is that the consequences of erroneous actions are left to fall squarely upon those whom have made the errors, and consequently do not weigh on those who have not. Conversely, those who have made good decisions are allowed to fully enjoy the benefits of their actions. The education of men as to which actions are advisable and which are to be avoided is progressive and ongoing.

Who sets the rules? By definition, there are no rules apart from what has been mutually agreed upon by consenting parties. That said, it is easy to imagine how quickly a myriad of rules may spring forth in a truly capitalistic society. The key difference between the mutually agreed upon rules and those imposed by governmental decree is that compliance with the agreed upon rules under True Capitalism is voluntary, making compliance far more likely. For to violate the rules of an agreement is to forfeit the advantage imagined to be gained by entering into the agreement.

Even the primordial requirements of the right to life and property would organically be honored, for they are primordial to all humans, whether they readily admit it or not. Being primordial, the securing of both life and property would be amongst the first series of contracts that any person would seek to enter into, whether directly or indirectly. Were society allowed to progress to such a point, it may take the form of tacitly understood mutual peace accords between every member of society. It is not so difficult to see, through this lens, that this myriad of small-scale peace accords would be preferable to reliance upon the fickle peace accords entered into by nation states with standing

NATURAL LAW AND THE THEORY OF ECONOMIC SYSTEM FLUIDITY: MARX AND RAND TOGETHER IN PERFECT HARMONY

militaries.

Despite the ability to freely enter into agreements at one's own discretion, all of mankind is completely subject to natural (or divine, as one prefers) law. While all humans are subject to the demands of these immutable laws, it is True Capitalism that allows for the fullest and most complete expression of the operations of natural law to guide the actions of men.

THE NATION STATE'S CAMPAIGN AGAINST TRUE CAPITALISM

To fight True Capitalism, mankind's least flawed response to his surroundings, is to cause or submit to chaos and misery. Yet every nation on the planet is working to some degree towards hindering the natural operation of True Capitalism within its domain.

Why would the current system of nation states act in opposition to a system that is beneficial to the whole of mankind? One reason for this is that the nation state, under the guise of being the most perfect expression of man's good intentions, today occupies the role as chief arbitrator between men. Another, perhaps more sinister reason, is that the existence of the nation state is portrayed as a sort of Robin Hood, a faceless bureaucracy which legitimizes the otherwise indefensible action of taking from some and giving to others. While the poor imagine that they are receiving from the rich, the nation state more often than not operates in a

NATURAL LAW AND THE THEORY OF ECONOMIC SYSTEM FLUIDITY: MARX AND RAND TOGETHER IN PERFECT HARMONY

manner that enables the rich to receive from the poor.

It should now be clear that the role of both chief arbitrator and Robin Hood could be fulfilled in a much more efficient and just manner by allowing True Capitalism to operate unhindered. However, the leap from the presumption of being protected from others to full trust in others is, for many, an impossible one to make.

As the system of True Capitalism is essentially in direct competition with the nation state, it is only natural that the two systems would be the antithesis of one another. Where the nation state regulates by edict, True Capitalism regulates by example. Where the nation state is rigid, True Capitalism is pliable. Hence, where True Capitalism will bend but never break, the nation state is repeatedly smashed to pieces when faced with change.

Moving to a more practical level, how can one be certain that True Capitalism is best suited to form the basis society? The proof lies in the fact that nation states, the institutions which supposedly offer the best option to that of embracing True Capitalism, are beginning to succumb to the punishments they have built up in their losing fight against it.

True Capitalism is now trumping the nation state, and the phenomenon that is currently playing out in Greece and throughout Europe will play out in nearly every western democracy as the nation state is shattered under a mountain of debt and broken promises. When the nation state breathes its last, True Capitalism, the system that has been there all along, waiting patiently to be acknowledged, will rush in to fill the void left by its collapse.

Thankfully, natural law will not change, and one does not have to wait for the collapse of the nations to begin living in harmony with it. Rather than spending an inordinate amount of time and effort willfully complying with every bureaucratic whim of the nation state, one's time could be better spent understanding the immutable truths of natural law.

Understanding and working in harmony with natural law will not only assist in complying with the demands of the nation state when called for, it will prepare the adherent to operate in a world where the nation state no longer exists.

TRUE CAPITALISM VS. MIGHT MAKES RIGHT

True Capitalism is the economic system that is mankind's most productive response to the state of anarchy in which it finds itself. Far from being an undesirable reign of chaos, Anarchy, the absence of government, is the natural state of man. If anarchy is simply a natural state that cannot be altered, then it is man's response to Anarchy that must be examined, not Anarchy itself.

In response to this natural state, man has two options: He can choose to mutually cooperate with his fellow man, respecting both his fellow mans' right to live and his right to property, or he can choose to lay claim to his fellow mans' life and property through the use of force.

In other words, man may choose the path of True Capitalism or might makes right. Ideologically, there is no middle ground. In practice, men live at various points on the spectrum between these two extremes.

In the previous chapter, it was shown that the system of nation states that is the basis of the current international system is incompatible with the truly capitalistic system. The reason for this incompatibility is that the ideological basis upon which all of the nation states on the planet have come into existence, the principal of might makes right, is the ideological antithesis of True Capitalism. As such, the nation state's actions tend to hinder the efforts of its citizens to respond to the incessant demands of natural law.

No matter how much freedom a nation state may allow its citizens, it must be recognized that the nation state stakes its claim on the individual's life at birth, by declaring them a citizen and, in many cases, requiring either military service or registration to be conscripted into military service should the nation state deem it necessary. The nation state then stakes its claim on the individual's property through either taxation or a myriad of rules and regulations regarding the use of said property. More commonly, both methods of confiscation are employed.

Far from being an ultimate given, the nation state, at its basic level, is a created entity that provides varying levels of security and welfare services. What differentiates the nation state from other agencies providing security and welfare services (such as security firms and insurance companies) is that the nation state enjoys a geographic monopoly which it enforces by both the threat and use of violence against both foreign invaders as well as what may be accurately described as its captive audience, otherwise known as citizens.

NATURAL LAW AND THE THEORY OF ECONOMIC SYSTEM FLUIDITY: MARX AND RAND TOGETHER IN PERFECT HARMONY

This is the world today, and any sober look at the facts will lead one to conclude that mankind has chosen to pursue might makes right as the dominant response to its anarchic natural state.

Yet there is a better way. True freedom and prosperity can be found almost immediately by merely embracing True Capitalism and abandoning the might makes right doctrine. In contrast to might makes right, the act of changing mankind's response to Anarchy from the doctrine of might makes right to True Capitalism cannot be achieved by resorting to violence, for by definition, resorting to violence is simply a furthering of the might makes right response, not a legitimate step towards a truly capitalistic society.

Rather, the only type of revolution that would naturally bring about a truly capitalistic society involves rejecting all aspects of the might makes right doctrine. It involves renouncing any and all choices which make use of violence, whether undertaken personally or by directing the nation state to use violence on one's behalf, to take the life or property of another while at the same time asserting one's rights to have their own life and property respected as inviolate.

In practice, this type of revolution would take place peacefully by adhering to the doctrine of non-resistance. This revolutionary doctrine is further expounded upon in the great works referenced in Volume I.

THE CHARACTERISTICS OF A TRULY CAPITALISTIC SOCIETY

What would a truly capitalistic society look like? On the surface, a truly capitalistic society may not look that different from the current structure of things. There may arise security and insurance companies that serve geographical areas in tandem in such a way that they closely resemble the current nation state structure. However, assuming that the paradigm is changed and man truly embraces truly capitalistic ideology, nobody will be compelled under the threat of violence to be a client of the security or insurance company. Rather, individuals who choose to hold property would be free to choose between defending and securing their own property and income streams or voluntarily contracting with the security and insurance companies for these services.

In a truly capitalistic society, the division of labor would flourish and the property and resources would quickly pass from unproductive hands to

NATURAL LAW AND THE THEORY OF ECONOMIC SYSTEM FLUIDITY: MARX AND RAND TOGETHER IN PERFECT HARMONY

productive hands, organically balancing the competing goals of maximizing output and capital preservation.

Companies who abuse their clients would quickly be abandoned and weakened while those who deliver the best service and value to their clients would prosper and attract more clients. This rule naturally applies equally to security and insurance companies in stark contrast to the monopoly on these services currently claimed by the nation states of the world.

The lack of compulsion under the threat of violence is the key difference between the ideologies of True Capitalism and might makes right. The doctrine of might makes right naturally engenders fear and evokes a response to others based on this fear. True Capitalism engenders, encourages, and rewards trust and evokes a response of trust in others. It is upon this inherent basis of trust that a truly free and prosperous society blossoms.

The choice between True Capitalism and might makes right is one which must be made. The world's anarchic state demands a response, and these two options are the only responses known to mankind. All other supposed choices are simply points on the spectrum between these extremes, but the choice of guiding ideology determines the direction that mankind and societies are gravitating towards along this continuum.

The ideologies of True Capitalism and might make right are opposing magnets, and remaining at a point in between them on the continuum is not an option, for society is always being pulled in one direction or the other depending upon the dominant ideology adopted by the majority at any given time.

If mankind is to live in peace and toil successfully in response to the demands of natural law, the pull of the magnet of True Capitalism must be the more powerful of the two in the hearts and minds of the majority. It is not simply a question of economic philosophy; it is a matter of life and death.

SECTION II - NATURAL LAW

NATURAL LAW: THE TRANSCENDENTAL IMPORTANCE OF SUPPLY, DEMAND, AND EQUILIBRIUM PRICES

Before diving into the broad subject of natural law, a brief review of section I will greatly aid the context in which natural law is being approached in this volume.

In section I, it was established that Anarchy, the lack of government, is mankind's natural state. It is an ultimate given, and a clear understanding of the current state of affairs depends upon grasping this inescapable fact.

In response to Anarchy, mankind has two choices. He can choose to mutually cooperate with his fellow man, respecting both his fellow man's right to live and his right to property, or he can choose to lay claim to his fellow man's life and property through the use of force.

In other words, man may choose the path of True Capitalism or might makes right. Ideologically, there is no middle ground. In practice, men live at various points on the spectrum between these two extremes.

True Capitalism is the response which creates the greatest benefits to society in terms of peace, security, capital accumulation, and material prosperity while the ideology of might makes right, by definition, is the antithesis of True Capitalism and consequently would create the greatest detriment to society.

Ironically, all of the nation states in existence derive their power from the adoption of the might makes right ideology by a majority of the people. How, then, can one be certain that True Capitalism is the proper response to Anarchy if the majority has clearly embraced the doctrine of might makes right?

The proof of the superiority of True Capitalism is that it allows man to best adapt and react to the inescapable demands of natural law. Like Anarchy, natural law is immutable. It simply is. Mankind is bound to it whether the majority chooses to recognize it or not. It does not change, for its statutes are etched in the foundations of the earth itself. It is as Ayn Rand stated: *"You can ignore reality, but you can't ignore the consequences of ignoring reality."*

For purposes of this exploration, the reality that Rand refers to in the above quotation is natural law. Natural law may be ignored, but ignorance of it always comes at a price.

The first of the two immutable natural laws with

regards to economic systems is that of supply and demand. The law of supply and demand holds that supply of and demand for a good or service will tend to find a point of equilibrium at a certain price expressed in monetary terms. The price relationship is referred to as the equilibrium price. On a graph the relationship looks like this:

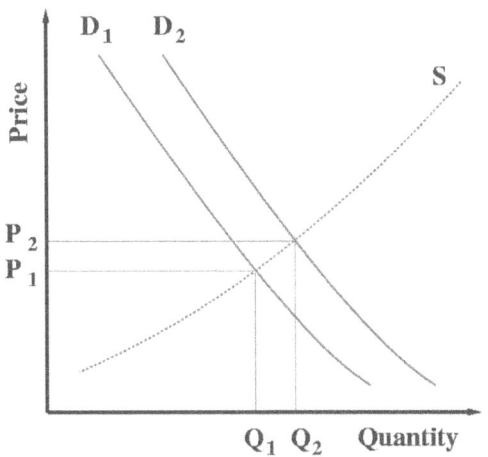

A Graphical illustration of the price and quantity relationship embodied in the Law of Supply and Demand - Source http//:commons.wikimedia.org, user: CSTAR http://commons.wikimedia.org/wiki/File:Supply-demand-P.png

In simple terms, the law of supply and demand is a way of expressing what most people intuitively know. When an item is increasing in price, one of two things is happening. Either people are demanding more of the good or service or the supply of the good or service at the previous equilibrium price point is diminishing.

Naturally, the opposite is also true. When a good or service is decreasing in price, one of two things is happening. Either people are demanding less of the good or service or the supply of the good or service at the previous equilibrium price point is increasing.

In either case, the change in the price of the item in monetary terms is providing crucial information to all of those either producing or consuming the good or service in question, for it serves as a guide for their inherent speculations.

*{**Editor's Note:** Speculation, far from being an illegal or immoral activity, is essential to everyday survival and without it, there is no hope of achieving equilibrium prices and therefore both production and consumption tend to either carry on at a suboptimal level or, in certain cases, cease altogether. It is important to clarify that the illegal or immoral speculation that is villianized in the media today is generally the act of investing the money of another party in certain types of speculative ventures without the knowledge or consent of the other party to do so.}*

As a producer, if one sees the price of the good or service that one provides increase, the he or she will strive (or speculate, as it were) to either increase production to take advantage of the opportunity to profit and/or others will strive to produce the good or offer the service for which the price is seen increasing.

As a consumer, if one sees the price of the good or service that one consumes increase, the he or she will strive to either decrease consumption to mitigate the effects of the higher prices or others will strive to find a less expensive substitute for the good or service to offer in the place of the good or service for which the price is increasing.

As production increases and substitutes are brought to market, the law of supply and demand operates to counter these changes by locating a new equilibrium price based on the new dynamics of the supply of and demand for the good or service. The increase in production serves to increase supply that, as the natural law of supply and demand dictates, will eventually lower the equilibrium price as the corresponding demand is satisfied. Likewise the decrease in demand will have the same effect of increasing the available supply.

In either case, the individual decisions and speculations of both the producers and consumers serve to increase the available supply. The process occurs tacitly, and is an example of what Adam Smith famously called the invisible hand of the market.

To further sum it up in a phrase that may at first seem a paradox, the best cure for higher prices is higher prices.

There are no exemptions from the natural law of supply and demand, however, there are numerous examples of nation states, guided by the principal that might makes right, manipulating the pure message that the equilibrium price of an item is intended to send to producers and consumers.

This manipulation may be achieved in overt ways, such as price controls that set the price of an item by way of a decree. However, most people understand that price controls are not beneficial. As price controls do not enjoy popular support, today's nation states commonly resort to other tactics to achieve similar ends. Amongst these tactics are taxes, subsidies, and the granting exclusive privileges to either buy or sell the good or service in question via regulating the purchase of or granting monopolies for its production.

Regardless of the tactic employed, the end result is always a manipulation of the equilibrium price for the good or service and as such, serves to distort the price signals that guide the speculations and ultimately the actions of all producers and consumers. The end result of price manipulations for society as a whole are always and in every case suboptimum outcomes when compared to those that would be achieved if the price signal were allowed to be transmitted to all actors in a pure form.

As taxes, subsidies, and tariffs are imposed by nearly every nation state in existence, one can only imagine the level of economic confusion occurring in the world today.

In the case of central banking and centralized currency controls, the nation state, in addition to the normal tools of price manipulation mentioned above, adds the further complication of manipulating the price of the monetary units that the equilibrium prices are expressed in. This further distorts the price signal that is universally relied upon to direct the actions of producers and consumers.

The true capitalist ideology, on the other hand, completely subjects itself to the law of supply and demand and, in return, provides producers and consumers with the best opportunity to obtain and act on the most accurate price information available.

To solve the problem of price manipulation via the price of the monetary units, a truly capitalist society quickly settles on a common currency (which is more often than not denominated in a set standard measure of gold and silver) and does not recognize the right of anyone to tax, regulate, or grant monopolies. As such, a truly capitalist society continually works to bring supply and demand into balance in the simplest, most efficient way possible: By relinquishing the illusion of control over economic activity to the market.

In a truly capitalistic society, inefficiencies are naturally wrung from the system as firms that depend upon the false price signals or special protections or subsidies provided under the might makes right ideology quickly go out of business.

True Capitalism not only serves to eliminate economic waste, it quickly directs the surplus capital into its most urgently needed employ, and it accomplishes this by way of obeying and embracing the natural law of supply and demand.

THE GOLDEN RULE

While society appears infinitely complex on the surface, the foundation is extremely, perhaps painfully simple once it is reduced it to its base elements. Any complexity that mankind experiences is not a product of an inherent complexity in natural laws, rather, it is a product of the human relationships and actions that are a result of mankind's choice of responses to the demands of natural law.

True Capitalism is mankind's best response to the demands of natural law, for it tacitly operates to create the greatest benefits for the greatest number of people. The proof of the superiority of True Capitalism is that it allows man to best adapt and react to the inescapable demands of natural law.

After the law of supply and demand, which deals with how to best make use of the scarce natural resources of the earth, there exists a second natural law with regards to economic activity that primarily governs human relationships. It is popularly called the Golden Rule, and it is designed to work in conjunction with the law of supply and demand.

The Golden Rule is articulated and exalted as an ideal in some form in nearly every society and religion on the planet. The Bible famously articulates the Golden Rule in the following way in the book of Deuteronomy chapter 6, verse 5:

"Love your neighbor as you love yourself"

It is important to note that the Golden Rule is a positive declaration. It is a call to action. In many societies and religions the Golden Rule is stated in a negative declaration, and is adopted in the form of a command to abstain from certain actions. An example of this can be found in Hinduism:

"One should never do that to another which one regards as injurious to one's own self." - Anusasana Parva, Section CXIII

This negative declaration is sometimes called the Silver Rule. It is important to understand that only the Golden Rule, the positive call to action, is natural law. Unlike the Golden Rule, the Silver Rule does not rise to the level of natural law; rather, it is a logical corollary to the Golden Rule.

Compliance with the Golden Rule, as with all natural law, is indispensible. It is ignored at one's peril, for it operates regardless of one's acceptance of its validity or not. The truly capitalistic society greatly facilitates and encourages compliance with the Golden Rule. Conversely, compliance with the

Golden Rule is characteristically hindered in a society that has embraced might makes right as its preeminent response to mankind's anarchic surroundings.

The idea of the Golden Rule being natural law may be hard to grasp. This difficulty arises because the Golden Rule is largely ascribed to religious observances.

The essence of natural law is that it is universally true and applicable to all. The law of supply and demand, for example, can be ignored for a time. However, as Ayn Rand's observation alluded to earlier, every moment of ignorance causes the consequences of that ignorance to accumulate further until a final breaking point is reached.

The result of the failure to comply with the law of supply and demand is material scarcity and ultimately death. This fact is clear to most. However, it is less clear that the same is true of the Golden Rule. Every instance that the Golden Rule is ignored in the affairs of mankind causes the consequences of ignoring the Rule to accumulate further until a final breaking point is reached. In the case of the Golden Rule, the result of the failure to comply is by definition a failure to properly comply with the law of supply and demand as well, with the end result, as mentioned above, being material scarcity and ultimately death.

Compliance with the Golden Rule is a necessary prerequisite to compliance with the law of supply and demand, for the Golden Rule governs relationships in the purest sense. So broad are the implications of the Golden Rule that the origins of both the rule of law and more recently the concept of human rights can be traced to it.

What thrusts the Golden Rule out of the realm of being simply a good idea and into the realm of natural law is this: All attempts to comply with the Golden Rule serve to coordinate the actions of men in such a way that the greatest number of human needs are met in the most efficient way. Any deviance from the Golden Rule, by definition, is a failure to meet human needs in the most efficient way. Again, by definition, failure to meet human needs in the most efficient way means that a greater number of human needs are simply not being met.

Far from being simply a moral standard, the Golden Rule is fundamental in the determination of supply and demand. As the equilibrium price serves as the beacon of production for the law of supply and demand, the actions taken by men, governed by the Golden Rule, initially determine the supply and demand factors which, when combined, produce the equilibrium price. In this sense, the Golden Rule serves as the beacon for both supply and demand, the elements that allow an initial equilibrium price to arise.

AN EXAMPLE OF THE OPERATION OF THE GOLDEN RULE

Each human being has needs and wants which are sources of uneasiness. Human action, to paraphrase economist and philosopher Ludwig Von Mises, consists of men and women acting to dispel their most intensely felt uneasiness. If a man is hungry, he will direct his actions towards getting something to eat. Other tasks will be put on hold until this intensely felt uneasiness is relieved.

The operation of the Golden Rule, in the example of the man's need to alleviate his hunger, operates in the following way. First, a man feels hunger. Upon acknowledging this need, he has two options before him with which to fulfill this need. The first option open to him is to forage, hunt, fish, or perform any series of actions towards the end of fulfilling this need. The second option is for him to voluntarily cede some of his production (or production for others via his contribution of labor) or appeal to the charity of someone else in return for something to eat. As the second option above is nearly always the most expedient, it is likely that a majority of people will elect this option.

Now reflect upon the Golden Rule: *"Love your neighbor as you love yourself."* The person who chooses to comply with the Golden Rule will quickly understand that if he has the need to be fed, it is likely that his neighbor (in this sense, neighbor would mean anyone in the geographical realm in which he is equipped to serve, up to every person on the planet if it is possible for him to serve them) is likely to have the same need to some degree. With this revelation, he unwittingly is on his way to discovering the crucial element of demand.

As he seeks to voluntarily fulfill this demand, he will either need to produce the supply of food himself or he may voluntarily cede some of his production (or production for others via his contribution of labor) or appeal to the charity of someone else in return for a supply of food with which to provide his fellow man with something to eat. The aggregated action of any number of people matching their productive activities to meet the demand for food, if left unhindered, will serve to provide an adequate and relatively uninterrupted supply of food in optimal quantities for all who freely participate in exchange.

In this example, which could apply to any good or service desired by mankind, the information obtained by producers with regard to the needs of his fellow man via adherence to the Golden Rule will serve to guide their speculations as to where to best employ the limited time and capital of a society.

It is a simple example, yet its simplicity serves to highlight the operation of the Golden Rule and can apply to any situation regardless of the complexity. The Golden Rule, in modern business school lingo, is the origin of market research; it is the impulse for entrepreneurial activity, and it forms the basis for all subsequent human actions.

THE QUESTION OF CHARITY

The prior chapter's explanation of the Golden Rule begs that the question of charity be briefly addressed. The question of charity is the following: Would not universal adherence to the Golden Rule quickly lead to widespread scarcity and bankruptcy as catering to everyone's preference to receive something for free would quickly deplete all available supplies and production?

The answer to the question of charity lies in the Golden Rule itself: *"Love your neighbor as you love yourself."* Most persons are not keen to provide something to someone without the assurance or at least faint hope of receiving compensation, either directly or indirectly, for their actions.

As such, it would hold that only those who are in a position to give something away and are willing to do it would choose to engage in purely charitable giving. Further, if all members of society were striving to comply with the Golden Rule, the norms of charity would then fall under the governance of the law of supply and demand.

The beauty and perfection of the Golden Rule is that above all it demands balance in human relationships and by extension, balance in the supply and demand of material goods.

TRUE CAPITALISM ENABLES COMPLIANCE WITH THE GOLDEN RULE

Another weakness of the might makes right ideology upon which modern nation states are founded is that it gives rise to the assumption that individual compliance with natural law is optional. While at best, might makes right may rely upon the Silver Rule to govern human relations, True Capitalism completely subjects itself completely to the Golden Rule and, in return, most accurately directs human actions towards fulfilling the most urgently felt needs of the greatest number of people.

As stated above, True Capitalism causes inefficiencies to be naturally wrung from the system at their source as errors are quickly corrected and information is quickly disseminated to all participants in a trade via equilibrium prices. The proper identification of demand, by default, leads to the most efficient allocation of scarce resources that is possible under current conditions. The tacit guarantees of respect for life and private property that are enabled by the truly capitalistic system allow mankind to supply this demand by employing their limited time and resources without unnecessary hindrances.

The Golden Rule may not provide everyone with what they expect or desire, but complete submission to the Golden Rule not only guides society towards the most efficient allocation of resources, it gives mankind the best available information on which to base their attempts to mutually cooperate in order to most efficiently attempt to fulfill what is a myriad of human desires.

More importantly still is the fact that adherence to the Golden Rule has the added social benefit of creating the greatest amount of harmony and goodwill possible in human relations.

THE THEORY OF ECONOMIC SYSTEM FLUIDITY: MARX AND RAND TOGETHER IN PERFECT HARMONY

Despite the superiority of True Capitalism as a response to the demands of natural law, it is clear from observation that socialism, the economic system implied as a result of the might makes right ideology, is widely championed and practiced at one level or another. Indeed, the fact that all nation states owe their existance to the principles of might makes right serves as proof that a majority of mankind holds to the belief that the world would be a better place were the socialist system to be widely adopted and adhered to by all of mankind.

In the realm of economic thought, there are two extremes. On one end of the spectrum sits the economic equivalent of Karl Marx's workers' paradise, known as socialism. On the other end sits the economic expression of Ayn Rand's rugged individualism, known as capitalism. As anyone who has studied these philosophical extremes can tell you, daily life for most people occurs somewhere in the space between these two philosophies, making strict adherence to either both impractical and indefensible.

While apologists for these extreme positions do a wonderful job of explaining why complete adherence to their ideals by all would lead to an utopia on earth, a careful examination of the arguments, along with a quick glance at how things operate in the real world, lead one to conclude that evidence of both the socialist and capitalist ideals can be found in nearly any functioning economic system.

How can this be? If the extremes are both correct in their reasoning, they must be mutually exclusive of each other. However, as one looks at the world around, as well as into the depths of their own souls, they invariabley find an uncomfortable coexistence of ideals that is difficult, if not impossible, to reconcile.

That is, until now.

The Theory of Economic System Fluidity serves to elucidate and reconcile this age old dilemma. The theory is simple: Socialism appears to work for and can be tolerated by local systems, while large scale systems are best served by embracing capitalist ideals.

Socialism, with its embrace of community property and centralized decision making, is in many ways a superior policy to that of capitalism for

NATURAL LAW AND THE THEORY OF ECONOMIC SYSTEM FLUIDITY: MARX AND RAND TOGETHER IN PERFECT HARMONY

systems until they reach a certain critical mass. Part of the reasoning for this is that socialism unwittingly provides the framework in which society cares for its economically weaker members. It is a system which is entered into with the understanding that at least a portion of one's actions will take the form of altruism, that is, they will work for the benefit of others without the expectation of material compensation. In fact, socialism is the basis for the family unit through which a great deal of humanity enters the world.

Given the barbarities which are justified in the name of profit, it can be said that the basis for morality and human decency is most frequently observed and celebrated in a socialist setting. Given the inherent requirement of altruism, socialism is the system which constantly asks the individual to look beyond themselves. However, socialism on a large scale tends to bring out the worst in human beings, as the inevitable onset of poverty quickly diminishes any moral advantage that small scale socialism may have enjoyed.

The question of morality must be tabled for the moment to interject an insight with regards to the corporate legal structure. Corporations, entities which are generally held out as the bellweathers and champions of capitalism, are, in fact, socialist institutions. It is for this reason that employee wages do not fit well into free market pricing mechanism and instead lend themselves to the "Labour theory of value" which is a base concept of socialist philosophy.

The logical proof of this is the following: The

employer/employee relationship is based on a set pay rate per time period of work performed. Once it has been agreed upon, the wage rate ceases to adhere to free market theory and becomes merely a component of the Labour theory of value. The top level managers in corporations that employ persons in an employee capacity become the centralized authorities in what is a defacto socialist realm.

Another further proof that corporations are socialist entities is found in the fact that any property which is held in the name of the corporation is generally cared for and used by employees to some extent. As such, corporate property, as its name would imply, is held in common by subjects who themselves have no property rights in said property. They may be offered shares in the corporation themselves, but this does not directly effect their day to day use of the corporation's (their employer's) real and personal property.

A majority of human beings alive today will find themselves born into and later employed by a socialist entity of some sort, be it a family, household, corporation, or governmental employer (which, for purposes of analysis, behaves in a similar fashion to a corporation), and it is within these systems that a majority of mankind experiences most of its day to day interactions. It is understandable, then, that most people would see a form of socialism as the logical basis for a utopian ideal.

However, the members of these same socialist organizations which have direct interactions with actors outside of their corporate realm, the heads of

NATURAL LAW AND THE THEORY OF ECONOMIC SYSTEM FLUIDITY: MARX AND RAND TOGETHER IN PERFECT HARMONY

household, CEOs, heads of government, members of boards of directors, salespeople, security personnel, customer service agents, and a host of others, well know that the *"esprit de corps"* which may exist in their organization is thrown aside in their dealings with the outside world. The outside world, where individual corporations collide in fierce competition, is marked by brutal self interest and the protection of private property rights which are the hallmarks of capitalism.

Capitalism, the system which honors private property rights and glorifies the pursuit of self interest, must be embraced and allowed to operate in an unhindered state as the basis for the interactions between the small scale socialist systems (families, corporations with employees, and those brave individuals who choose to face the anarchic system of the world alone.)

The reason that capitalism must be embraced by the smaller systems is that its principles, namely respect for life and private property, best enable mankind to confront the incessant demand of the natural laws of supply and demand and the Golden Rule. Compliance with the demands of these natural laws must be allowed dictate mankind's day to day activities so that the smaller systems can better adapt and survive in what is at its base a harsh, unforgiving, and anarchic environment.

However, apart from its invaluable contributions to understanding the material world, even hard core capitalists would agree that blind adherence to the capitalist creed may not only lead to the trampling of those less fortunate in society, but also the potential isolation of the individual from human warmth, feeling, and the concept of love.

For all of the virtues of capitalism, its potential frigidness at the individual level and lack of a clear moral compass make it largely unpalatable to the majority as an absolute ideal.

The Theory of Economic System Fluidity is the only rational way to understand the interplay between the systems that otherwise would give rise to irreconcilable differences between the ideologies. The Theory of Economic System Fluidity holds that socialism tends to operate and thrive on a small scale, while capitalism operates on a large scale as a matter of necessity. As the theory of biologos attempts to bring harmony to the polarization of two views of the world's origins, the Theory of Economic System Fluidity allows the economist and politician to embrace both the virtues of the Socialist ideal as well as the Capitalist economic imperative.

Were this theory available to either Karl Marx or Ayn Rand as it is now to their modern day disciples who choose to accept it, one can envision a scene where Marx crosses the room and asks Rand to dance, she accepts, and suddenly, in the midst of their waltz, the world begins to make sense.

The final question which the Theory of Economic System Fluidity seeks to answer is the following: In terms of size, at what point is it appropriate for a system to cease to be predominantly guided by socialist principles and break up into units better able to cope with its anarchic surroundings? In other words, when must a socialist system cede its ideology to the dreaded the capitalist model not by choice but out of economic necessity?

The answer to this question naturally defines the size limitation of what may be called a functional socialist system. While there is no firm, numerical answer in terms of absolute or relative size, it is clear that a socialist system has reached its limit when it is corporately bankrupt and unable to fulfill its commitments, either morally or financially, to its members.

When a corporation reaches this point, it must adjust its productive activities and/or release either property or employees into the capitalist system until it finds a new point of equilibrium. The released employees would then find themselves, albeit for a moment, in what may be called the free market for labor. In it, they will either learn to compete perpetually in the capitalist environment and form their own small scale socialist entity, or link up quickly with another socialist entity, be it another corporation, state welfare, or the generosity of a family unit.

The fact that both families and corporations can accumulate wealth are proof that socialist entities can and do compete and thrive in a world where capitalist thinking and political structures are imperatives. Ultimately, it is the ability of each socialist unit to constantly adapt to an ever changing social and economic landsacpe and to seize opportunities which may present themselves. The degree to which a socialist unit is able to sucessfully adapt will ultimately determine its success or failure.

History has shown that when socialism is

employed on a large scale, it tends to lose both its ability to compete economically as well as any moral superiority which it may have enjoyed. When persons are thrust headlong into poverty, which is the logical economic end of large scale socialism, what were once moral imperatives are tossed aside in pursuit of what are purely capitalistic aims in a desperate attempt to survive.

Anyone who has lived such an event will attest that it is in these unfortunate circumstances that the rotten core of humanity is laid bare for all to see. While unbridled capitalism has its own faults, which are daily brought to light in the media as a reminder of when the ideology has been allowed to run too far, it is this collective consciousness,together with the innate human desire for mercy that are constantly at work to keep the evils of capitalism from dominating the human experience.

The beauty of the Theory of Economic System Fluidity is that the normal operation of each system keeps the proliferation of the other in check, so fluid is the interplay between the systems that any attempts by government or sovereigns to impose or preserve one system over the other will eventually end in either frustration or disaster.

CONCLUSION

It is increasingly important that mankind take adequate time to pause and reflect as to what ideology is being tacitly or actively pursued as a guide for its daily toils. As the collective efforts of mankind reach an effectiveness that was unimaginable a generation ago, the throws of human action are having a profound impact not only on an increasingly interconnected global economy, but also on the very earth which mankind has been entrusted with.

It is no longer a safe assumption that the natural world can perpetually work to unilaterally correct mankind's mistakes. A deep examination of each person's motives in light of the Golden Rule is desperately needed to ensure a prosperous future for many.

On one hand, the key to material prosperity lies in allowing mankind to tacitly coordinate its varied productive efforts by adhering to the ideals of True Capitalism in large scale dealings, for it is the ideology which best allows mankind to respond to the incessant demands of natural law. Yet the blind pursuit of material prosperity promises a future in which the human experience degenerates into a state that is devoid of compassion and mercy.

On the other hand, an espousing of many facets of the socialist ideal at the most intimate levels of society is evidence that mankind is keenly aware of the need for human warmth and compassion. However, if human warmth and compassion is allowed to trump efficient efforts towards satisfying needs and wants, mankind will quickly run short of both warmth and compassion in a mad scramble to survive.

The key to understanding the virtues of both the socialist ideal and the much villainized but indispensible ideology of True Capitalism lies in understanding that they are both incompatible with one another and at the same time can peacefully coexist. This same understanding can be found in the Theory of Economic System Fluidity, which explains how both systems are uniquely equipped to fulfill what on the surface appear to be competing human needs. The Theory of Economic System Fluidity allows for both True Capitalism and socialism to be practiced in a peaceful equilibrium so long as persons are not hindered from voluntarily choosing the amount of time and resources they will dedicate to the pursuit of each system during their lifetime.

While both socialism and capitalism hold that their approach to satisfying the natural law of supply and demand is superior to and more just than that of the other, the Theory of Economic System Fluidity allows for the natural law of supply and

NATURAL LAW AND THE THEORY OF ECONOMIC SYSTEM FLUIDITY: MARX AND RAND TOGETHER IN PERFECT HARMONY

demand to operate on the competing economic systems themselves, permitting mankind to seamlessly redirect its efforts towards the ideals of one system or another as their conscience and the incessant demands of natural law may dictate in a way that strict adherence to either the socialist or capitalist dogmas could never hope to replicate, even under the best of conditions.

Above all, mankind must abandon the might makes right ideology which is the ideological core of the modern nation state. For while the unhindered operation of True Capitalism leaves ample room for socialist enterprises to operate within its structure, the might makes right ideology serves only to hinder the operation of both economic systems with the end result being a poverty stricken society devoid of human warmth and compassion. A world where might makes right is truly the worst of both worlds.

The ultimate virtue of True Capitalism is that it allows both for mankind to collectively respond to the demands of the natural laws of supply and demand and the Golden Rule by means of tacit, peaceful cooperation. Within this framework, mankind can then voluntarily form and disband units based on socialist ideals in a peaceful manner.

The Theory of Economic System Fluidity is the only way to understand the interplay between the systems that otherwise would give rise to irreconcilable differences between the ideologies. Socialism operates on a small scale, capitalism on a large scale, Marx and Rand dance a beautiful dance, and mankind waltzes its way towards the utopian ideal which is each system's high and noble aim.

Pacioli's Gift or Bernanke's Curse?

How Mankind's Greatest Innovation has Enabled Its Greatest Catastrophe

Volume VI

PACIOLI'S GIFT OR BERNANKE'S CURSE? HOW MANKIND'S GREATEST INNOVATION HAS ENABLED ITS GREATEST CATASTROPHE

VOLUME VI

CONTENTS

An Introduction	240
Dual-entry Accounting: Pacioli's Gift to Humanity	243
The Presumption of a Monetary Constant	247
Irony: Dual-entry Accounting Creates Central Banking's Architecture	252
The Role of Government as an Enabler of Central Banking	255
The Poisoned Money Supply: A Clear and Present Danger	259
Money or Credit: What's in Your Wallet?	262
The Dawn of Modern Central Banking	265
Central Banking Ushers in the Sunset of Civilization	267

The Absence of Natural Limitations on Human Actions	271
Free Banking: The Ultimate Solution	275
Free Markets Need Free Banking: The Lakota Solution	280
Conclusion	283
Appendix A: Silver for Bitcoins: A trade for Digital Sound Money	287
Appendix B: Why Short-Term Interest Rate Management is Harmful to the Economy: The Unseen Funding Dynamic	291

AN INTRODUCTION

In response to what has become known as the Financial Crisis of 2008, the Central Bankers of the world have employed nearly every form of monetary alchemy at their disposal in a desperate attempt to maintain the status quo. The status quo, which in this case means that all commercial banks and sovereign governments remain both liquid and solvent, has become increasingly difficult to maintain as each attempt to stimulate economic growth via ultra low discount rates and quantitative easing has seen a diminishing marginal return in terms of economic growth. The longer the Central Banks of the world engage in these and other forms of financial alchemy, which in the end serve as futile attempts to defy immutable natural laws, the greater the danger of a complete economic collapse becomes.

The unconventional measures employed by the Central bankers of the world over the past five years are not only failing to achieve their stated goals of

PACIOLI'S GIFT OR BERNANKE'S CURSE? HOW MANKIND'S GREATEST INNOVATION HAS ENABLED ITS GREATEST CATASTROPHE

increasing employment and economic growth, they are triggering what is quickly becoming an unmitigated disaster in fixed income markets. These markets, once the bedrock of global finance, have now been conditioned, in the Pavlovian sense, to do nothing more than attempt to front run the actions of the Federal Reserve and other Central Banks up and down the yield curve.

The action that is taking place in the financial markets is akin to a 300-pound man, who represents the Central Banks, chasing an 800 pound gorilla, which represents the financial markets, around on a queen sized waterbed. The action is becoming completely unpredictable and extremely dangerous. Throw in the chaotic interventions of a 10 pound Chihuahua, who represents the sovereign governments' meddling in the financial market mechanisms via commercial banking regulation and tax policy, and the entire situation is a basement flood waiting to happen.

As the chaos on the waterbed, which is a metaphor for the accumulated wealth of mankind in the real world, continues to unfold, it is important to examine and understand, to the extent possible, how humanity has arrived at this critical juncture in history, where a fat man chasing a gorilla while dancing around a Chihuahua on a waterbed can threaten to damage the wealth of nearly everyone on the planet.

It is the aim of this volume to answer this question by exploring two of the oft overlooked elements that have, each in their own way, given rise to the system which enables a relatively small group of persons the ability to destroy the accumulated wealth that is the result of mankind's 9,000 years of toil. These elements are commonly known as Dual-entry accounting, which we refer to as mankind's greatest invention, and Central Banking, which we refer to as mankind's greatest catastrophe.

After exploring these elements, we present the concept of Free Banking as the antidote for the curse of Central Banking, and the ultimate solution to the current and future financial crises that the world will suffer at the hands of well meaning Central bankers who, it would appear, are oblivious to the destruction that their chosen profession mercilessly inflicts on humanity.

DUAL-ENTRY ACCOUNTING: PACIOLI'S GIFT TO HUMANITY

First we will explore Dual-entry Accounting, which, despite the many groans it has caused to be uttered by first year business students, is nothing short of mankind's greatest innovation. In order to understand the simple logic and profound impact of Dual-entry Accounting on our modern world, we must first travel back to Venice in the year 1492.

In 1492, Venice is the center of the western world and Christopher Columbus has just set sail from Galicia to find a new trade route to India. While Columbus' "discovery" (it is possible that when Columbus passed away, he remained under the impression that he had discovered nothing more than outlying islands en route to India, not the giant land mass that until then was unknown to Western Civilization) of the Western Hemisphere has had lasting impacts on both sides of the Atlantic which are still being felt today, a discovery that was far more universally beneficial was being recorded by a

Franciscan monk by the name of Luca Pacioli at his monastery in Venice. A discovery so astounding that it would later be called *"a catalyst that launched the past into the future" (Luca Pacioli: Unsung Hero of the Renaissance, by: Jackson, Tinius, Weis, South-Western Publishing Company, 1990)*.

As Columbus unwittingly sailed for the new world, Pacioli sat down in his simple room to create the outline for his treatise on mathematics: *Summa de Arithmetica, Geometrica, Proportioni et Proportionalita (The Collected Knowledge of Arithmetic, Geometry, Proportion, and Proportionality)*.

As part of what threatened to be the first in the long line of boring textbooks dealing with mathematics, Pacioli saw fit to include a section entitled *Particularis de Computis et Scripturis* (Details of Accounting and Recording) in which he described the accounting practices used by merchants in Venice at the time. When Pacioli's *"Summa"* was finally published in 1494, it contained what is recognized as the first complete description of Dual-entry Accounting.

Pacioli's work in *Summa* made him a nearly instant celebrity. He was invited to Milan to teach and counted none other than Leonardo Da Vinci amongst his pupils. Da Vinci and Pacioli became friends and the understanding of proportions that Pacioli passed on to Da Vinci were employed in the mural "The Last Supper" and a number of Da Vinci's later works. *Summa* was one of the first books published on another game changing innovation that was birthed in the Renaissance, Gutenberg's printing press. To this day, Pacioli is known as "The

PACIOLI'S GIFT OR BERNANKE'S CURSE? HOW MANKIND'S GREATEST INNOVATION HAS ENABLED ITS GREATEST CATASTROPHE

Father of Accounting."

To be clear, accounting in some way, shape, or form has always been practiced. What Pacioli accomplished, perhaps unwittingly, was to disseminate throughout Europe the accounting methods that had made the merchants in Genoa, Florence, and Venice the most successful in the Western World.

What makes Dual-entry Accounting so special? Dual-entry Accounting, in a nutshell, is the formal recognition that every trade has a net affect on the income statement and balance sheet of an individual or enterprise.

This method of recording transactions of economic substance enabled merchants and producers to understand which of their daily activities created wealth and which did not, allowing them to make informed decisions regarding which activities to undertake with their limited time and resources.

While this now seems intuitive, it is hard to overstate the benefits that the dissemination and use of Dual-entry Accounting has bestowed on Western Civilization by way of enabling a greater number of persons to engage in activities which increase the capital stock, and consequently the accumulated wealth, of society and allowing them to more quickly abandon activities which deplete this accumulated wealth. This facilitation of wealth generating activities is why Dual-entry Accounting may be considered man's greatest innovation.

Yet, in perhaps the greatest irony that the economic world has ever known, Dual-entry

Accounting has enabled the very existence of man's greatest catastrophe, Central Banking. How did this bitter irony come to pass?

THE PRESUMPTION OF A MONETARY CONSTANT

Luca Pacioli was first and foremost a mathematician. He understood that mathematics relies upon certain constants to remain, well, constant in order for the calculations that depended upon them to be meaningful. Whether or not Pacioli was conscious of the fact, implicit in his presentation of the methods of Dual-entry Accounting is the assumption that the monetary units in which merchants and producers kept their accounts was a stable or sound monetary unit. The presumption of a sound monetary unit, meaning that the monetary unit holds a stable relative value over long time horizons, implies that Pacioli wrote with the understanding that money is to the economic world what constants are to the world of mathematics.

Also implicit in this presumption was that the monetary units that were used as units of account on the accounting ledger contained a constant weight of silver or gold that existed in the natural world. Silver and gold that had been hewn out of the ground and struck into coinage of a set weight and metallic alloy by the men at the old Zecca, the Mint of Venice in the Rialto district which preceded its famous successor which was completed in 1545.

This was an important presumption, as the Dual-entry Accounting method only works when the accounts are in balance. The numbers on the accounting ledgers were understood to represent physical goods or claims on physical goods. Therefore, the balance of accounts in the physical world implies that physical goods are in existence or are reasonably expected to come into existence and become available for exchange.

When Pacioli penned *Summa*, the Venetian Zecca was one of the largest and most reputable mints in the world. This reputation was born in no small part of a scandal at the Zecca which consummated with the Doges, who ruled Venice at the time, issuing a decree on the 11th of November, 1457 against then noted variations in the weight and purity of the gold and silver coins that the Mint at Venice had produced. As a result of this renewed commitment to monetary purity, the coins that circulated in Pacioli's time and locale, the Silver Ducat, Soldo, Lira Sequin, and Gold Ducat, served as the standard of trade in the world known to Pacioli and his contemporaries.

Given that the Venetian merchants could count on this sound monetary standard on which to base their accounts and, by extension, their choice of activities, their use of Dual-entry Accounting not only benefited their own interests, but had the side effect of benefiting all those who traded in the

PACIOLI'S GIFT OR BERNANKE'S CURSE? HOW MANKIND'S GREATEST INNOVATION HAS ENABLED ITS GREATEST CATASTROPHE

Venetian coinage, whether or not they, too, had mastered the art of Dual-entry Accounting. For the use of sound money ensures that mankind's activities are constantly brought into balance with the natural resources at its disposal.

For those merchants and producers who had mastered the art of Dual-entry Accounting in this environment of sound money, the ability to properly recognize and record their transactions and to make sense of the results gave them a sort of super power. This super power, the ability to recognize the value of transactions over longer time horizons and therefore direct investments over longer time horizons, was further refined by Pacioli, who employed the use of Arabic numerals and proposed a system of mercantile accounting that could apply uniformly to all trades and nations.

However, Dual-entry Accounting, as mankind is now coming to understand, is a two edged sword. For Dual-entry Accounting to work in favor of those who practice or rely upon it, the monetary unit of account must hold a stable value over long time horizons. The presumption of the relatively stable value of the monetary unit in relationship to the natural world is essential for interpreting the primary output of Dual-entry Accounting, the profit or loss signal. The stable unit of account is also essential when evaluating the worth and employment of items that are represented by entries to the balance sheet, upon which the profit or loss signal ultimately depends.

In short, the stability of the monetary unit of account is essential if Dual-entry Accounting is to be relied upon for sound decision-making.

For the Venetians, this requirement was met by virtue of their relatively stable monetary unit. As such, the Venetian Mercantile class rose to dominate the Western world. Indeed, with few notable exceptions, Dual-entry Accounting has rendered an invaluable service to mankind and has allowed human progress to follow a generally upward trajectory in terms of material well being ever since Pacioli made his bequeath to mankind.

As a stable monetary unit enables the super powers of Dual-entry Accounting to operate, an unstable monetary unit, of which there are numerous examples in the largest economies in the world today, circa 2013, is its kryptonite. A monetary unit that does not have a relatively stable value over long time horizons, specifically the time horizons required for large scale investments of capital to be planned with the precision required for them to be successful, serves to render the gift of Pacioli powerless.

In doing so, an unstable currency threatens to take mankind from the comfort of their large screen televisions, sofas, and smart phones, and throw them back into the dark ages, from which the world that Pacioli lived in had recently emerged. It threatens to take Pacioli's gift and make it "*a catalyst that launches the future into the past.*"

In the irony of ironies, mankind has, for the past 100 years, made use of Pacioli's gift to create the largest system of unstable money, commonly known as fiat currency, that the world has ever known. This disastrous employment of the super powers of Dual-entry Accounting is known as Central Banking, and it has quickly turned the world's economies into a series of unmitigated catastrophes waiting to happen.

IRONY: DUAL-ENTRY ACCOUNTING CREATES CENTRAL BANKING'S ARCHITECTURE

Now that we have explored the often underestimated contribution of Luca Pacioli to the commonwealth of society, we are prepared to deal with the irony that Dual-entry Accounting, man's greatest innovation, has made possible the widespread dissemination of man's greatest catastrophe, Central Banking.

We will accomplish this by presenting a brief history and explanation of the concept of Central Banking and its unique relationship to sovereign government.

The concept of Central Banking is deeply rooted in man's need for security as well as recognition of his co-dependence on the activities of his fellow man. While the romanticized ideal of the yeoman farmer still persists to some extent today, it is generally recognized by most humans that the best

PACIOLI'S GIFT OR BERNANKE'S CURSE? HOW MANKIND'S GREATEST INNOVATION HAS ENABLED ITS GREATEST CATASTROPHE

way to increase one's well being is through the operation of the specialization and division of labor and resultant trade amongst parties.

However, the emergence of trade brings with along its own set of difficulties that demand a solution. As it takes time and energy to obtain and protect wealth in this world, it also takes time and energy to barter with counterparties while trading differing goods without a suitable means of exchange.

The profession of banking has sprung up organically to assist those engaged in production with the means to both protect and easily exchange their excess produce with others. A bank, in its simplest form, provides a secure place to store wealth away from one's own property. A natural extension of this activity is for the banker to extend credit and act as a clearinghouse for commerce by assuming a de facto role as an issuer of currency in the form of banknotes, which represent a claim on wealth held at the bank on behalf of others. The existence and circulation of these banknotes has indeed greatly facilitated trade.

As trade and consequently the wealth of mankind increased both in volume and geographical reach, there was increasingly a need for a larger banking interest to store the excess wealth of the individual banks and to honor the banknotes emitted by the individual banks. This larger banking interest, formed by and for the benefit of the individual banks, is what we today call a Central Bank.

The complexity of maintaining bank accounts was greatly facilitated and made possible on a large scale by the use of Dual-entry Accounting. In turn, the ability for individual banks to maintain accounts on a larger scale has made possible the existence of Central Banks to act as a clearinghouse amongst banks. Hence, Dual-entry Accounting has unwittingly enabled large-scale Central Banking, man's greatest catastrophe, to come into being.

Yet it is not Central Banking alone that causes its machinations to wreak havoc on mankind. For a Central Bank, without the means to exercise a monopoly on the composition of the money supply, is held indirectly accountable to its mission of safeguarding assets by society's merchants, producers, and laborers.

However, once a Central Bank is granted a monopoly over the composition of the money supply, a monopoly that can only be provided by a sovereign government, it ceases to defer to the interests of the merchants, producers, and laborers, and becomes preferred tool of the subjugation of society by those who find themselves at its helm.

THE ROLE OF GOVERNMENT AS AN ENABLER OF CENTRAL BANKING

We will now explore the role of government in relation to Central Banking. For once a government grants the exclusive power over the composition of the money supply to a Central Bank, a symbiotic relationship is formed between the two that becomes lethal to the society over which both exert their specific form of influence. The Central Bank exercises primacy in the monetary realm while the government exercises primacy in the realm of physical security.

As Central Banks arose in response to mans need for someone to look after his wealth and facilitate trade, governments arose because man needed someone to look after his life and ensure that the peace be maintained to the extent possible. Governments, then, were formed in response to man's need for a common defense.

To most, it seems like a foregone conclusion that one would assent to abide by the rules of a certain government and pay some form of tribute to the government in exchange for the preservation of one's life and the general peace in society. However, recognizing the ideological origin of human government is important when understanding why a government and Central Bank always find themselves in a symbiotic relationship, meaning that one cannot exist without the other.

Governments, in whatever form, have come to rely heavily upon and generally supported the formation of both individual banks and Central Banks. Why would governments need banks and Central Banks to exercise their authority?

The answer lies in the impossibility of balancing the intangible benefits of maintaining the peace with the economic demands of the peace's daily maintenance. Governments are generally given license by the members of society to use whatever means necessary to preserve their lives. As such, government assumes the role as the apparatus of compulsion and coercion in that society.

As the apparatus of compulsion and coercion, the government, by definition, cannot generate wealth through its activities. At best, it can only create the conditions under which its subject individuals may create wealth, but the activities of government as a provider of security never directly create wealth. Because the government cannot create its own wealth, it must either borrow from or tax the populace in order to fund its activities.

The Central Bank, as the ultimate repository of wealth, offers a convenient source of both credit and, in a later wave of Central Banks of which the Federal Reserve is a prime example, tax collection services.

The Federal Reserve: Storage of Wealth and Tax Collection Services provided with a smile

As you can see, a Central Bank is an indispensible institution both for individuals in terms of storing wealth and facilitating trade, as well as for governments, that have an insatiable need for tax revenues and credit.

However, the existence of a Central Bank, for all of the benefits that it may bestow to a society, unwittingly makes the wealth of those it serves a natural target for plunder. Central Banking, like alcohol and socialism, may be a good idea when used in moderation, however, each Central Bank that exists represents a large-scale economic catastrophe waiting to happen. For if the circumstances under which the bank operates take an unfavorable turn, the wealth and livelihood of many may be lost in a very short period of time.

Needless to say, the scale of Central Banking circa

2013 is beyond what would be advisable, and the potential for catastrophe is unprecedented.

How, when, and most importantly, why will this catastrophe take place? We can only answer the why, and we will tackle it in the following chapter. The how and when are up to historians to decide, for those who live through it will scarcely have time to digest what is occurring, and, like the return of Jesus of Nazareth, it could occur at any moment.

THE POISONED MONEY SUPPLY: A CLEAR AND PRESENT DANGER

Why, then, will the current system of Central Banking come to an end that will cause wealth destruction on a scale that will make the weapons of war seem like child's play by comparison?

The answer, in simple terms, is that money, as it is widely understood today, does not really exist.

You read correctly. What a majority of the developed and semi-developed world uses as a store of wealth, unit of account, and medium of exchange is a figment of the collective imagination.

It is generally understood today that the value of money is not necessarily in money proper, which exists in coin, paper, and digital form, rather the value of money is found in the ability of the bearer to exchange said money for goods and services. What is often overlooked in this observation is that, for money to be exchanged for something of value between willing participants in a transaction, the item that which is used as money in the transaction must be universally perceived to have a certain value that is easily transferable between the parties.

Following this logic, what society uses as money is, by definition, simply another good which is widely recognizable as useful in exchange and therefore carries a price premium (which is often referred to as the monetary premium) of a certain amount, which is usually far above what some economists would incorrectly* call the good's intrinsic value.

{Editor's Note: Value judgments, while often influenced by what are known as market, or intrinsic values, are by definition made by the individuals who willingly enter into a transaction, not disinterested observers. It is for this reason that it is more accurate to appraise value by observing price points of transactions on the margin (i.e. transactions that are actually taking place) as opposed to appraising value based on past transactions or transactions imagined to take place in the future. Many are the hypothetical gains and losses of those who refuse to enter into transactions because they are waiting for an offer that is closer to recent market prices or that better matches what they perceive to be the intrinsic value of an item.}

Regardless of the monetary premium that a good may carry, whatever is used as money, by definition, must be a tangible good. Otherwise, we are dealing with credit, which is a promise to pay in money at a future date. Credit may be given in exchange in the place of money and is often traded at a discount to money delivered immediately, however, credit and money are two entirely different beasts.

While the distinction between money and credit

is assumed to be common knowledge, it is important to make a clear distinction in order to properly understand what will happen next as the catastrophe unfolds.

MONEY OR CREDIT: WHAT'S IN YOUR WALLET?

For a majority of roughly 9.000 years of human history, it has been tacitly agreed upon that silver and gold, usually in coin or bar form, are the highest and most widely recognized goods used as money. Further, it has been generally understood that the accumulation of silver and gold represent wealth.

As you may recall, the concept of banking and, by extension, Central Banking, arose in response to the need for man to protect his wealth. You may further recall that in order to both protect wealth and facilitate trade, a Central Bank creates banknotes that represent a claim on the wealth being protected by the bank.

The banknotes that the Central Bank creates are, by definition, credit and not money proper. Central banknotes are generally the highest and least discounted form of credit that are accepted in trade, but this does not change the fact that the banknotes are essentially credit and thus carry an implied risk of default. This risk of default places the ultimate limit on the circulation and acceptance of the banknotes that are used in trade at any given time.

From time to time, when a Central Bank's ability to protect the wealth entrusted to it came into question, banknotes would be presented directly to the Central Bank to be redeemed for the amount of silver and gold that they represented. If the Central Bank could not redeem the amount of silver and gold represented by the banknotes presented to it, the Central Bank was considered to be in default and, as word of the default spread, the banknotes in circulation would trade at an ever-increasing discount to real goods.

This logic further supports the fact that banknotes are credit, subject to default risk, and not money proper.

To cite just one modern example of the extent to which the number of Central Bank notes exceeds the amount of wealth in terms of gold reportedly held by the Central Bank, we will use data from the Federal Reserve Bank, the current Central Bank of the United States of America.

As of March 20, 2013, the Federal Reserve had issued $1,132,556,000,000 worth of banknotes, which, using the fixed price of $42.2222 of Federal Reserve notes per ounce of gold, which was set near the same time the Federal Reserve ceased to redeem its notes in terms of gold, those $1,132,556,000,000 worth of banknotes represent claims equaling roughly 26,823,708,854 ounces of gold. However, the Federal Reserve reports that it has only 261,499,000 ounces of gold in custody as of 2012, less than 1% of these theoretical gold claims.

While it may be considered a moot point that Federal Reserve notes are no longer redeemable in gold at the Federal Reserve Banks, it is important to understand that even if the Federal Reserve were to demand the current market price of gold, which is roughly $1,600 as of this writing, it would be able to redeem only 37% of the outstanding banknotes. This represents a substantial disconnect between the amount of wealth being circulated in the form of banknotes and the actual amount of physical wealth that exists inside the Federal Reserve's vaults.

Anyone who works for, trades, or saves Federal Reserve notes is a de facto customer of the bank. The statistics presented above indicate that two out of three customers of the Federal Reserve have been defrauded, or, presented another way, all of the Federal Reserve's customers will have lost two thirds of their wealth in the real world. Either way one looks at it, once the status quo can no longer be maintained, this fact will become evident to all who have entrusted their wealth to the Federal Reserve and other Central Banks of the world by virtue of holding their savings in the form of central banknotes.

Can you now sense the scale of the impending catastrophe? Or, to put the question more directly: What's in your wallet?

THE DAWN OF MODERN CENTRAL BANKING

Today, the scale of modern Central Banking is unprecedented, as is the potential for a currency related catastrophe. The reason for the unprecedented scale of modern Central Banking is that money, as it is widely understood today, does not really exist. Rather, banknotes issued by Central Banks, which are by definition credit instruments, are misunderstood to be money proper by a majority of the people in the developed and semi-developed world. We refer to this phenomenon as the *"Poisoned Money Supply."*

This misunderstanding flies in the face of nearly 9,000 years of human history, in which gold and silver in bar and coin form have been tacitly used as money proper. It is this misunderstanding which has set the stage for perhaps the greatest catastrophe in history to occur. How and where did mankind go so terribly wrong in its choice of money?

The misunderstanding of money and credit began, like many modern day social experiments, in Northern Europe with the establishment of the Bank of Amsterdam. Established in 1609, the Bank of Amsterdam is widely recognized as at least a precursor to modern Central Banks. For over 400 years since the Bank of Amsterdam was established, the use of banknotes issued by a Central Banks that are not directly convertible to precious metals has slowly but steadily increased throughout the globe.

Modern Central Banks issuing banknotes were subsequently formed in other European countries, as well as in England and Japan. As these Central Banks and their successors began to slowly absorb the true money supply and issue banknotes in their place, mankind began to slowly transfer the concept of money proper from gold and silver and attribute the qualities of money exclusively to the banknotes issued by the Central Bank. This process has gone on largely unhindered, as the existence of a Central Bank has generally been seen as a societal advancement.

CENTRAL BANKING USHERS IN THE SUNSET OF CIVILIZATION

The process of wealth absorption greatly accelerated in 1913 when the United States of America granted a 100 year charter to its third Central Bank, the Federal Reserve. The FED, as it is commonly known, was to act primarily as a guardian of reserves and to create "money" (read banknotes) as necessary. At the advent of World War I, the FED stepped in and issued bonds to finance the Nation's war efforts. After the war, the FED was granted exclusive control of the Nation's money supply. This was the first nail in the coffin of the economic engine of the United States.

In 1933, in the midst of what was later to be known as the Great Depression in the United States, then President Franklin D. Roosevelt signed Executive Order 6102 which required citizens to deliver all but a small amount of gold coins and bullion held by them to the FED in exchange for $20.67 worth of Federal Reserve notes (the banknotes issued by the FED) per ounce.

Naturally, most citizens with large quantities of gold at the time had it physically transferred to Switzerland.

Then, by decree, the Government raised the price of redeeming gold at the FED from $20.67 to $35 per ounce. Additionally, redemption could only be made by foreign parties as, naturally, it was now illegal for US Citizens to own large amounts of gold. Almost overnight, Federal Reserve notes had become the only form of "money" that an entire generation of Americans was likely to handle. While foreign parties had the ability to redeem the Federal Reserve notes for gold at $35 per ounce, they rarely did. The second nail in the coffin of the policies, or more accurately, beneficial lack of policies, that had made the United States the economic center of the world, had been hammered down.

After World War II, the US emerged as the most powerful nation on earth. It was only natural that the Western governments would peg their currencies at a fixed exchange rate to the US dollar (Federal Reserve Note) which the governments could redeem in gold at $35 per ounce should the need arise. This international currency arrangement is commonly known as the Bretton Woods system.

The Bretton Woods system held together for around 20 years, operating under the assumption that $35 US dollars were as good as an ounce of gold until 1968. Then, in the late summer months of that year, the unthinkable happened.

The unthinkable occurred on a quiet August afternoon in 1971 at Camp David. It was a time not so unlike our own.

PACIOLI'S GIFT OR BERNANKE'S CURSE? HOW MANKIND'S GREATEST INNOVATION HAS ENABLED ITS GREATEST CATASTROPHE

The Vietnam War was becoming increasingly unpopular and the social climate was ripe for protest. The US, thanks to the economic distortions introduced by the poisoning of its money supply, had run up a large and increasing trade deficit with the rest of the world. It was becoming clear that if foreign dollar holders were to redeem a significant amount of their Federal Reserve Notes, which we now understand to be credit and not money proper, for gold, which we now understand to be money proper, the FED would not be able to deliver enough gold and the insolvency of the Central Bank which underpinned the financial system of the entire world would be revealed.

The solution that came forward to help the FED avert an embarrassing open default was to gradually increase the amount of Federal Reserve Notes required to obtain an ounce of gold from $35 to $41 between 1968 and 1971. Then, in 1971, with the US dollar collapsing in value and the Bretton Woods system falling apart at the seams, then President of the United States Richard Nixon announced that US dollars were no longer convertible into gold. This event is now referred to as the Nixon Shock.

And a shock it was. The Federal Reserve had effectively defaulted. The US dollar, the benchmark of Central Bank issued currencies throughout the world, was now officially backed only by the faith that it would continue to be accepted in trade. Most of the world still lives by this faith today, and if anything, the delusionary faith in banknotes issued by a Central Bank which has defaulted on its obligation to deliver real money on demand has only grown.

However, the reason that the large scale catastrophe of modern Central Banking still lies ahead is that over the past 40 years, the lack of gold and silver to back the banknotes in circulation has been conceptually replaced by the expectation that governments, and by extension their citizens, will produce enough goods and perform enough services to repay the obligations represented by the banknotes.

Unfortunately, this expectation will never be fulfilled. The unrestricted quantity of banknotes and obligations to deliver banknotes in existence will always tend to exceed the stock of available goods and services that can be delivered in exchange. In fact, the existence of the credit based monetary system in operation today is dependent upon an exponential expansion of debt.

These debts will never be repaid, for they have their origin in boundless human desires that, by default, come into being without the means to fulfill them. As the expectations placed upon both the people and their governments are increasingly defaulted upon, the natural societal outcomes will be bitterness and hostility. The bitterness and hostility will be intensified by the perceived lack of basic resources in the material world.

The period of time, which we refer to as the catastrophe at hand, will seem to many like the sunset of civilization. In many ways, this will be an accurate assessment.

THE ABSENCE OF NATURAL LIMITATIONS ON HUMAN ACTIONS

Human beings are fallible. It is normal and should be expected that they will not be able to deliver on certain obligations. The natural beauty of banknotes redeemable in gold and silver is this: If it is suspected or observed that a person or entity would be unable to pay on their obligations, a creditor would move to seize the gold, silver, or other assets that the debtor had pledged as collateral.

The seizure of collateral or the threat of seizure is often enough to correct the failed human action or decisions that were leading to the net loss of wealth incurred by the activity that had been undertaken. In economic parlance, we would call this the correction of the malinvestment of resources.

Without gold and silver to act as a natural limitation on the supply of banknotes and other forms of credit, the bad decisions that lead to the malinvestment and the activities that lead to the destruction of wealth and resources can continue, unchecked, for a very long time.

The use of gold and silver as money had another, more important function that is often overlooked. Gold and silver are inert, non-consumable objects. Their hoarding and use as money will not generally cause starvation or want. In fact, the hoarding of gold and silver as money would have the effect of lowering general prices as productivity increased, naturally creating an incentive to decrease production which in turn would raise prices, making the expenditure, or de-hoarding, of more silver and gold necessary and in turn raise prices, creating a natural incentive to produce.

Gold and silver allow the economy to naturally regulate itself and, by virtue of the difficulty in extracting them, indirectly cause the rest of the earth's resources to be used in harmony with each other.

Finally, gold and silver are inanimate objects. Their recognition and possible seizure as collateral does not threaten the liberty or life of a person. However, because modern Central Banking has largely eschewed money proper and circulated credit in its place, it will become increasingly common to see entire societies held as security for a debt that many of them had no direct hand in creating. This is the tragic yet logical end of using credit as money.

It is the truth that will bring tragedy to the earth.

Without the natural counterbalance to trade and growth which gold and silver money had provided for over 9,000 years, man's activities, whether productive or destructive, have continued nearly

PACIOLI'S GIFT OR BERNANKE'S CURSE? HOW MANKIND'S GREATEST INNOVATION HAS ENABLED ITS GREATEST CATASTROPHE

unchecked for the past 40 years. It is staggering to think of the catastrophe that awaits us if we truly are on the path to destruction.

Mankind, by nature, is always on the path of destruction, and the use of gold and silver as money had previously been effective in correcting human action before mankind had strayed too far down it. With the advent of modern Central Banking, The mechanism that provided mankind with the means to auto correct itself has been removed.

Most people alive today have been trained to believe that using gold and silver as money is an unnecessary and environmentally harmful process. Even Adam Smith believed that if the time and effort expended to mine and mint metals as currency could be directed to other, more useful activities, all of humanity would be better off.

What Smith and others who hold to this idea fail to realize is that mankind would not always direct its energies to useful activities. Like modern Socialists, he underestimated the power of self-interest inherent in all human action. Today we are preparing to reap the consequences of 40 years of unrestricted and more often than not, misguided human actions.

While it may be too late to avoid the catastrophe that faith in modern Central Banking will bring upon us, it is comforting to know that a return to the understanding and use of gold and silver as money offers hope for a future of truly infinite possibilities.

Fortunately, Pacioli's gift, the dissemination of Dual-entry Accounting, along with the honorable intentions of bankers can be once again harnessed for good. The solution lies in the concept of Free Banking.

FREE BANKING: THE ULTIMATE SOLUTION

The concept of Free Banking is perhaps the most important thing that people today can dedicate themselves to, for it is the precisely a lack of freedom when it comes to currency and credit which has lead to stripping of the earth's resources and the resulting environmental problems which a number of developing nations suffer from in a disproportionate manner.

Specifically, the suppression of Free Banking in favor of modern Central Banking has caused the activities of man to create what is an unsustainable imbalance with the demands of the earth's natural systems.

So what is Free Banking? It is not a lack of monthly charges assessed to a consumer's bank account, as the name may suggest to many in the developed world, rather, it is the freedom for banks to openly compete as issuers of credit and safe keepers of currency in any form. It is a rejection of the Central Bank's monopoly on the issuance of coin and credit.

The current banking system, which is enslaved to the modern Central Banking model, has a fatal flaw in its design. Its fatal flaw is that banks are obligated to issue credit and accept deposits in currencies that are nothing more than debt issued by the Central Bank. This constraint causes the bank notes created by the Central Bank to become the basis of all of mankind's activities. This occurs out of necessity, as modern Central Banks have solidified their monopoly on bank note issuance in collaboration with their sponsoring government, which obligates its citizens to pay taxes to the government in Central Bank notes. This mechanism is embodied in laws relating to legal tender.

To compound this fatal flaw, the issuing Central Banks work to actively manipulate interest rates, which affect the price of the flawed currency and credit, making the value of both the credit and savings of everyone completely subject to the machinations of the Central Bank. In the gorilla and waterbed metaphor that we presented in the introduction to this volume, one can imagine the gorilla sitting peacefully on the waterbed, unmolested by the 300-pound fat man or the Chihuahua. Once the fat man jumps on the waterbed via interest rate manipulation, the chaos ensues. Ditto for the Chihuahua.

Why is interest rate manipulation, the primary tool of modern Central Bank policy implementation, ultimately harmful? Precisely because the manipulation of interest rates serves to throw the real, naturally occurring interest rate hopelessly out of balance with the true needs of the economy.

If the currency that everyone is working for had been created legitimately by the labor of another person and its price, via the interest rate mechanism, were allowed to respond to real supply and demand signals, a natural balance would be struck between both credit and savings in a society. This balance would express itself as conservation and eventual increase of the earth's resources and useful capital stock available for use in production.

However, the currency which everyone is currently working for is nothing more than a piece of data created by a computer and printed onto a piece of paper. To make matters worse, via the active manipulation of the interest rate mechanism, the currency is not allowed to be properly discounted in trade. As such, all of the labors of man are set towards destroying the earth, ultimately turning vital resources into more pieces of paper to be deposited into a bank in order to close out the credit account created by entries in a computer.

In recent years, we have observed the zeal with which Bolivia's Evo Morales and other revolutionary leaders have implemented wide reaching social reforms by closing down a majority of the ministries of the government almost immediately upon taking office. Closing ministries is a swift move in which a leader may quickly consolidate power. However, as one studies these cases, they will see that often there was one notable exception, an entity that is left untouched and is allowed to continue operating: The nation's Central Bank.

The reason for this is that a nation's Central Bank

is often seen as a sacred cow, even by those who vehemently opposite it, on the grounds that the currency and interest rates are too important to day to day life to be left in the incapable hands of the people, which is what the concept of Free Banking is all about.

However, it is for this very reason, the indispensible role of currency and credit in society, that currency and interest rates must not be left in the hands of any one entity, no matter how much clairvoyance or power over events is attributed to them.

No one would dispute the fact that grains and fuel are important to everyday life in nearly all the earth. However, even hard core Marxists would be hard pressed to admit that all peoples would be better off were only one entity given the ability to produce and set the price for either. As such, it has been proven over and over again that the expansion of the ability to produce such indispensible items not only serves to provide them in sufficient quantities to satisfy demand, it does so at a price that is more or less tolerable for all (this argument, of course, is null if the price is controlled by a single entity).

While free market proponents are quick to recognize the benefits of the universal freedom to produce grains, fuels, and healthcare, they often become hardcore Marxists when it comes to currency and credit. What those free market proponents who fall into this trap fail to realize is that all of the virtues of free markets are worthless if the most basic economic common denominators of currency and credit are not allowed to operate in a free manner, just as nature intended.

Free Banking allows free markets to solve all the problem of scarcity in currency and credit in the most efficient way possible. Why, then, do those in authority see Free Banking as the ultimate boogeyman? It is for one reason and one reason only:

Control of currency and credit represents the ultimate authority in the material world.

FREE MARKETS NEED FREE BANKING: THE LAKOTA SOLUTION

While free market reforms can go a long way towards liberating the peoples of the world, they are merely an expansion of the poisonous money supply if not coupled with a revocation of the Central Bank's monopoly on the issuance of currency and credit. Truly free markets allow both the banks and the people to choose in what currency or currencies they will issue credit and maintain their savings. Far from leading to anarchic chaos, the basic need for exchange and the issuance of credit amongst humans would cause all of society who wished to trade with one another to arrive at a tacit decision as to what is best suited to serve as currency.

While in most cases, this tacit decision has arrived on gold and silver to be used as currency, the most recent examples of empire, the British and American, grew so wealthy that lesser metals such as copper were thrust into use as currency.

As a practical matter, it must be admitted that

closing down the Central Bank of a nation would be a shock. For this reason, we look to solutions such as those seen in the actions of Canupa Gluha Mani, the Ithanchan of the Free Lakota Bank, as a path to Free Banking and the ultimate freedom of the peoples of the world.

The Lakota people declared their freedom from the Government of the United States in 2007. As an important part of this process, they knew that it would be necessary to establish their own monetary system. Further, they recognized that to simply choose another existing currency would again make them slaves to the creators of that currency.

To solve this problem, they opened the Free Lakota Bank and adopted what is known as the American Open Currency Standard, which is an attempt to return to a balanced system of metallic weights and measures that are recognized and traded internationally for use as currency in trade.

While this may seem now like an impossible step to take, the peoples of the earth must enjoy Free Banking if they are to enjoy liberty, private property, and equality before the law in any meaningful way. The lack of options in currencies in favor of the Central Bank's monopoly on the issue of credit will keep the peoples of the earth and their governments in the bonds of financial slavery until the Freedom of Banking is restored.

Free Banking, by its very nature, does not obligate a people to adopt a currency standard, as the native Lakota people have. While the most likely outcome of the liberation of the currency and credit markets is for all involved to quickly settle on a new, albeit more flexible, currency standard, it is necessary to guarantee that all peoples the right to choose which currency they want to hold and to bank in. This is the only way that man can live in harmony with one another and with the natural world. This freedom is the spirit of the principle of Free Banking.

CONCLUSION

While free markets and Free Banking represent mankind's best hope for averting disaster, many people look at the scene on the waterbed and side with the 300 pound man, who represents the Central Bankers of the world. After all, isn't he the only one taking action to capture and sedate the 800-pound gorilla, which in our metaphor represents the world's financial markets?

What this analysis fails to recognize is that the best course of action when dealing with an 800-pound gorilla is to observe it from a distance. Once the gorilla feels like it has an understanding of its surroundings, it will become docile and predictable unless it gets hungry or senses danger. If the gorilla gets hungry, one should let it find something to eat. If it senses danger, one's reaction should not be to calm the gorilla but rather to focus on the source of the gorilla's agitation and act accordingly.

The 800-pound gorilla is not the problem. In fact, it can often be counted on to recognize threats and, even though its reactions may seem unpredictable, gyrations in financial markets serve as early warning signs to potential economic problems on the horizon. Once recognized, economic imbalances can often be recognized and remedied before they become severe.

To silence the gorilla, or the gyrations in the financial markets, is to rob mankind of an important early warning system. Circa 2013, as the efforts of the world's Central Bankers to sedate the gorilla by force begin to escalate, many a Chihuahua (our metaphor's personification of the government) are being trampled and the waterbed of world economic activity is on the verge of springing any number of leaks.

This is an outcome that Luca Pacioli could not have envisioned, for he lived in an age and in a place where Free Banking and free markets were more or less givens. It was an age where capital formation was accelerating and the capital base from which we still operate today was being formed. All thanks to Pacioli's unwitting effort to disseminate the methods of Dual-entry Accounting throughout Western Civilization from his humble Franciscan abode.

While it is a great irony that a Franciscan Monk, sworn to poverty, would refine and articulate the greatest wealth generating innovation known to mankind, it is an even greater irony that this innovation would enable the large-scale employment of man's greatest threat to this wealth, modern Central Banking.

The unconventional measures employed by the world's Central Bankers in increasing measures over the past 100 and are not only failing to achieve their stated goals of increasing employment and economic growth, they are triggering what is quickly becoming an unmitigated disaster in the fixed income markets. These markets, once the bedrock of global finance, have now been conditioned to do nothing more than attempt to front run the central banks' interest rate cues up and down the yield curve.

Fortunately, the choice of whether to use Pacioli's gift for good or for evil is always at hand. Even as the world suffers under the grip of modern Central Banking, the ultimate solution of Free Banking, the banking that Pacioli and the Venetian merchants had assumed would always exist, is waiting in the wings to save mankind from its own penchant for error. In fact, Free Banking is not something that requires a great deal of compromise and administrative rule writing as most modern legislation does.

Free Banking operates under the rules of natural law, and it can be implemented via a simple political decision to get off of the waterbed and leave the gorilla alone.

Unfortunately, it is a political decision that modern governments, whose fate and existence depends upon the modern Central Banking model, will never take on their own. In the absence of political action, it will take the wholesale collapse of the Central Bank itself to rid the world of its menace.

It is the catastrophe to come, and it will leave the fortunes of many laid waste as it indiscriminately dismantles the erroneous divisions of labor and implied daily activities that it has caused mankind to organize itself under.

It is not a question of if, but when. For modern central banking will eventually give way to Free Banking out of necessity. When it happens, mankind will be allowed to continue its self-correcting path toward civility and peace.

And Luca Pacioli, if not Christopher Columbus, will be vindicated.

APPENDIX A: SILVER FOR BITCOINS, A TRADE FOR DIGITAL SOUND MONEY

*{**Editor's note:** The following is a redaction of an essay which first appeared on March 19, 2013, which explores the benefits of trading silver bullion for Bitcoins, as the Bitcoin's design and increasing acceptance make it the current gold standard of a coming wave of digital currencies. It is written in the context of the actions taken by the Cypriot government in exchange for financial aid from the European Union that was taking place at the time. These actions included freezing bank accounts in the island nation for over a week and imposing a heavy tax on all deposit in excess of 100,000 Euros. At the time of the writing of this volume, it was the harshest example of the moral dangers wrought by debt-based currencies issued by Central Banks, in this case, the Euro issued by the European Central Bank.}*

Silver for Bitcoins

As the events related to the European Union's proposed bailout of Cyprus continue to unfold, we have taken the decision to accept Bitcoins as a form of payment for Silver bullion products. While we accept that the Bitcoin, as a purely digital medium of exchange, is not without its risks, the mere prospect of a week long banking holiday, like the one the Cypriot banks are currently experiencing, occurring closer to home demands the creation of a contingency plan.

Being locked out of the bank, as the residents of Cyprus appear to be, can be downright lethal for commerce. Should the unthinkable happen in your neighborhood, it is essential to have a backup plan.

Owning silver bullion is the ultimate backup plan. Should the lights go out, silver is the most likely candidate to function as a medium of exchange once the inevitable chaos wanes into some sort of order. Should the lights stay on and one's bank accounts be randomly frozen by a government official, a more likely scenario in the near term, the ability to trade in Bitcoins will be essential for any merchant to be able to operate.

Will it work? Only time will tell. We can already foresee one possible glitch: Bitcoins have the distinct advantage of being anonymous. This is both their strength and weakness when it comes to selling bullion via mail, as in order to properly ship coins, this anonymity is likely to be temporarily relinquished into our care.

Beyond having a plan B should the banking system become "Temporarily Unavailable" on an individual or collective basis, in theory, accepting Bitcoins would be beneficial, as they should theoretically continue to appreciate in value against the fiat currencies of the world. The reason for this is that Bitcoin creation is set to occur on a fixed timeline and the number of Bitcoins created will be ultimately finite. As of this writing, Bitcoin adoption is running well ahead of the logarithm, which is currently causing massive deflation in terms of goods priced in Bitcoins.

Bitcoins are designed to be traded fractionally up to 8 decimal places. Should Bitcoin adoption continue to accelerate as more and more persons find themselves in need of a stable monetary unit in digital form, the rigid logarithm, which is Bitcoin's virtue, will not allow for the Bitcoin's continued use in commerce. The logarithm itself will not cause the cessation of Bitcoin transactions, rather, Bitcoins will be hoarded and therefore decrease in circulation. This has been described as its fatal flaw. When this occurs, the Bitcoin will, in theory, take its place in the digital realm as "Good money" in the terminology of Gresham's Law, and exit circulation. In its place will appear a plethora of digital currencies that would then come into existence via their own logarithm and trade against the Bitcoin on a relative basis as today's fiat currencies do.

In this sense, Bitcoin is the current gold standard of digital currencies. As such, the planned acceptance of Bitcoins for silver is like trading physical silver for digital gold, as Bitcoin's trajectory will theoretically track that of gold with one notable exception: Barring any subsequent changes to the logarithm, there will be no new "discoveries" of Bitcoins to augment the stock.

It seems like a good trade, and one we are willing to engage in to a point. However, it must be reiterated that wealth must be held in the real world to be of any worldly good, and trading in Bitcoins and other digital currencies, while temporarily solving the problem of rapidly depreciating fiat currencies, will serve to throw mankind's activities on the earth further out of balance with the demands of nature.

For man's activities to achieve balance with the earth, the monetary premium must be attached to something in the physical realm, not an inordinate amount of credit or data stored on servers. Besides, credits and data on servers have a strange knack for disappearing when you most need them. Silver coinage typically does not.

One last word to the wise, never, ever go short Bitcoins against fiat currencies, as doing so places one on the wrong side of a trade against a deep pocketed adversary: A fixed mathematical constant.

APPENDIX B: WHY SHORT-TERM INTEREST RATE MANAGEMENT IS HARMFUL TO THE ECONOMY: THE UNSEEN FUNDING DYNAMIC

*{**Editor's note**: The following is a redaction of an essay which first appeared on July 1, 2013.}*

The Unseen Funding Dynamic

Today, a revelation regarding the problem with fixing short-term interest rates (or any interest rate for that matter) came upon us. We believe that the revelation deals with both the problem of short-term interest rate fixing as well as the larger issue of the misplacement of the monetary premium, for the two are linked.

The revelation is the following: Imagine you are a banker who needs to fund a loan. In order to fund this loan, you would presumably need to have the money available with which to fund it. This is simple logic, however, in the real world of banking, the decision of whether or not to fund a loan is completely disconnected from the availability of funds, which is primarily determined by the overnight funding markets which, in turn, are completely reliant upon short-term interest rates.

In a world that followed the rules of financial physics, the short-term interest rates would be completely dependent upon the availability of funds in the system. However, the centralized management of interest rates makes this critical data point, which would otherwise provide a snapshot of the amount of capital in an economic system which is held in liquid form and available for deployment, irrelevant. Today, the amount of capital available in system can be determined on whim; such is the power of centralized discount rate management.

As such, the ability of the banker to fund the loan is not dependent upon an availability of funds that represents the amount of capital available in the real world; rather, his ability to fund the loan is completely dependent upon the borrower's ability to pay, the size of the loan, and the structure of the bank's balance sheet.

The three criteria above are important, as any underwriter will tell you, but the invisible fourth criteria, the true availability of the funds for the loan, what we call the funding dynamic, is completely ignored in the following fashion:

When the short-term interest is managed to be low, as is the case currently, any borrower who has the capacity to pay and has a lending need that fits well with a certain bank's loan mix is extremely

PACIOLI'S GIFT OR BERNANKE'S CURSE? HOW MANKIND'S GREATEST INNOVATION HAS ENABLED ITS GREATEST CATASTROPHE

likely to get funded, regardless of whether or not the economic system as a whole has the capital available to fund his or her loan. When the short-term interest rate is managed to be high, as it was in the early 1980's in the US, funding any loan, regardless of the ability to pay and fit with then bank's balance sheet, becomes impossible.

In both cases, both the borrower and the banker are left completely in the dark as to whether or not there exists the necessary capital stock or productive capacity in the economy for the funds to be deployed in the manner that the borrower envisions, for the short-term interest rate signal has been genetically modified to send a common signal to all participants.

Unfortunately, it is a signal that blinds everyone to the facts of the situation. For many are the hopes, dreams, and ideas of mankind, but it is the funding dynamic which keeps these hopes, dreams, and ideas in harmony with the natural world upon which we all depend.

Right now, we are floating in the clouds, completely disconnected from reality. The landing caused by the next round of high interest rates, via a natural rebalancing of accounts or further genetic modification of the short-term rates, will be very hard indeed.

The funding dynamic is so delicate that mankind cannot hope to optimize it via genetic modification, for when left alone, it is optimized by definition. Again, by definition, every attempt to modify will bring about sub-optimal results.

As with all complex economic and political

systems, dissent is information, and indirectly serves to manage the system's outputs while at the same time increasing the resiliency of the system, making it less susceptible to shocks.

Centralized short-term interest rate management must be abandoned before it is too late, for it is leading the activities of mankind towards a dangerous showdown with the limitations of the natural world.

To Build up the Land
Thoughts on Mankind's Uneasy Intercourse with Nature

Volume VII

TO BUILD UP THE LAND: THOUGHTS ON MANKIND'S UNEASY INTERCOURSE WITH NATURE

VOLUME VII

CONTENTS

Was the Land Created for Man? An Introduction	298
Man's Intercourse with the Land	301
The Division of Labor and the Concept of Trade	305
Maintaining the Peace	308
The Myth of Overpopulation	311
A Hard or Gentle People?	317
The Land Needs Rest	321
The Modern Challenge of Coordinated Rest	326
Conservation, What Occurs When Man Attempts to Control Rather than Build Up the Land	329
Agricultural Alarms: GMOs and CAFOs	333

Genetically Modified Organisms (GMOs)	335
Are GMOs a Form of Private Property or Pollution?	337
Confined Animal Feeding Operations (CAFOs)	340
Conservation Dooms the Land to Desertification	344
Why the Monetary Premium Must be Attributed to a Tangible Good	347
Conclusion	352
Appendix A: The Great Green Wall, and Are You a Soldier, an Athlete, or a Farmer?	356

WAS THE LAND CREATED FOR MAN? AN INTRODUCTION

Since the dawn of time, mankind has found itself obligated to perform a conjugal duty. The duty that we speak of is mankind's duty to the land. As with other activities that carry the same label, the duty is at times performed with joy or grumbling. In the worst of cases, the duty is not carried out at all.

This volume is an exploration of the increasingly distorted nature of man's intercourse with the land in which we live. The term "Climate Change" is commonly used to refer to the modern day observation of this distortion. However, climate change is simply the observation of the symptoms of what amounts to gross negligence on the part of mankind with regards to its conjugal duty to the land.

What is the conjugal duty owed by man to the land? To build it up.

Describing man's duty to the land in this manner, or even suggesting that mankind owe any duty to

TO BUILD UP THE LAND: THOUGHTS ON MANKIND'S UNEASY INTERCOURSE WITH NATURE

the land, may seem preposterous. Was not the earth created for the benefit of mankind? Is it not the land that owes a duty to us?

This volume is written from the point of view that both mankind and the land we inhabit have been created and were designed to be codependent. This point of view rejects evolutionary processes that, if taken as fact, leave both man and the land he inhabits utterly devoid of meaning.

It also rejects the idea that mankind remains in the utopia of the Garden of Eden, where the land merely renders its fruits to be unilaterally enjoyed by mankind. For it is clear from the creation narrative in Genesis that God first created the land, then plant life, with aquatic, avian, and land animals coming into being along the way. Mankind was created in the wake of the creation narrative. Further, while the narrative states that animal life was subjected to mankind, the land is never spoken of in the same sense.

In the Genesis narrative, it is only after the eating of the apple, the original sin and ultimate banishment from the garden, that mankind's relationship with the land is defined. Man is to till the land so that it will produce fruit, creating the codependent relationship between mankind and the land that exists to this day.

The most accurate origin and context for the points of view expressed in this volume, then, is from a place we will call "East of Eden," with apologies to John Steinbeck.

Somewhere to the East of Eden is where mankind first found itself pondering what it meant to till the land. It is a place where mankind, in its better moments, finds itself today.

MAN'S INTERCOURSE WITH THE LAND

"Then once more he raised his head, his face alive, his eyes far-focused, burning. He began to talk slowly, as though his lips were metal, stiffening. "The whole damn sandhills is deserted. The cattlemen are broke, the settlers about gone. I got to start all over-ship in a lot of good farmers in the spring, build up--build--build--"

- *Old Jules' dying words from the biography entitled "Old Jules" by Mari Sandoz*

With the inflationary fruits of five, nay, 100 years of loose monetary policy beginning to destroy the very currencies which gave birth to them, the world will soon be left to pick up the pieces and boldly move forward when all hope is lost. When there is no hope, one must fight to become hope themselves.

Fortunately, this is far from the first time that mankind has found itself in this situation. For inspiration, we look back roughly 100 years to a man who had a vision for a place that was then, as now, a place that is difficult to inhabit, the Sandhills region of Northwestern Nebraska.

That man is Old Jules.

Old Jules was a Swiss immigrant who settled in the rugged Sandhills and, as the title of this book implies, devoted much of his interesting life to "building up the land." What does it mean to build up the land? Your idea of building up the land probably means something quite different than my idea of building up the land, and we would both probably have visions quite different for building up the land than someone living 100 years ago as Old Jules did.

Yet all of our visions have merit, for the idea of building up the land, while it may manifest itself in any number of different ways, implies working with the land to help it produce.

The very idea of man being able to help the land to increase its production and that the land's production would, in turn, help mankind to increase their own production (or reproduction, to be precise), is a miracle. For those who inhabit urban settings, this intercourse between man and the land may seem like a mystery from a far off place.

Yet it is the result of two commands received by Adam and Eve at the dawn of creation. The first was before the fall, or what is commonly known as original sin:

God said, "Behold, I have given you every herb

TO BUILD UP THE LAND: THOUGHTS ON MANKIND'S UNEASY INTERCOURSE WITH NATURE

yielding seed, which is on the surface of all the earth, and every tree, which bears fruit yielding seed. It will be your food. To every animal of the earth, and to every bird of the sky, and to everything that creeps on the earth, in which there is life, I have given every green herb for food;" and it was so.

- Genesis 1:29-30

The second command, which has landed mankind where we are today, is a result of a curse placed on the land by God:

"...the ground is cursed for your sake. You will eat from it with much labor all the days of your life. It will yield thorns and thistles to you; and you will eat the herb of the field. By the sweat of your face will you eat bread until you return to the ground, for out of it you were taken. For you are dust, and to dust you shall return."

- Genesis 3:17-19

As we can see, man was initially meant to sit back and simply eat the fruits passively produced by the land. However, as a result of mankind's disobedience via the choice to partake of the forbidden fruit, mankind has been called into action.

As such, the current relationship between the land and mankind is one of an obligatory intercourse, if you will, with the fruit of one producing fruit in the other, and vice versa. Mankind's activities have become intimately connected to the land, and this connection has lead to what should be a mutually beneficial relationship. Mankind is to build up the land, and, in return, the land will build up mankind.

THE DIVISION OF LABOR AND THE CONCEPT OF TRADE

While toiling what we now understand to be a cursed land, mankind has become incredibly resilient an ingenious when it comes to building it up.

While the Victorian Yeoman farmer ideal may immediately spring to mind when one thinks of building up the land, it should be clear to thinking persons that the division of labor is a far more productive and resilient system by which to build up the land and to reap the benefits of such building.

Even in the Yeoman model, the division of labor existed. One fetched wood, another dug and plowed, another prepared food, still another built shelter, and another fetched water, and so on.

The division of labor could flourish beyond close knit communal groups, such as families or tribes, only via a system of trade. The concept of trade, which further enables the division of labor to operate, is important not only for the concept of building up the land, but also for the maintenance of peaceful relations amongst communal groups.

The link between mutual trade and maintaining peace between groups is as inseparable as the link between mankind and the land itself. In the words of Frederic Bastiat:

"If goods do not cross borders, soldiers will."

If all of these things, building up the land, the division of labor, and the necessity of trade, are to operate, the concept of money, or what is better described as the emergence of a good of the highest order which carries a monetary premium, must be tacitly agreed upon by all groups that engage in trade with one another.

Today, circa 2013, there is something desperately wrong with where the monetary premium is placed: Central Bank credits, or what most of us know as currency, or money. The problem is that they are debt, and not part of the natural world.

Since the monetary premium has been tied to debt, the operation of money, which should serve to build up the land, instead operates to tear it down. The very concept of money has been removed from the natural realm of coin, currency, or anything physical and naturally occurring, at least at a base level, and has been elevated and attached to the enigma of a debt, which exists purely in the imagination, if not aspirations, of men and women.

What many Keynesian trained economists praise as a triumph over the shackles of specie money, we lament as perhaps the ultimate delusion of our time. Such is the delusion that nary one in a million men

TO BUILD UP THE LAND: THOUGHTS ON MANKIND'S UNEASY INTERCOURSE WITH NATURE

will understand these words.

This disconnect between the monetary premium and the land, while giving rise to advances beyond our imagination, has thrown the earth's resources wildly out of balance via the unnatural transfer of the control of these resources into few hands.

The obvious effects of this purely monetary problem have led mankind to react to its effects on the environment by treating a limitless myriad of symptoms, the most extreme of which is the cry for conservation.

At its extreme, conservation seeks to completely cut off the intercourse of mankind and the land, ensuring the ultimate demise of both. What the land needs is neither the over zealous building up which takes place in the debt based monetary system, nor the sterile, hands off idleness called for by extreme conservationist agendas.

What both the land and mankind desperately need is balance. The only way to achieve this balance is to return the monetary premium to things that occur in the natural realm.

MAINTAINING THE PEACE

The monetary premium being primarily attached to something in that is naturally occurring is a precondition to achieving balance between nature and the activities of mankind. Another precondition for this is that mankind must live in relative peace with one another.

The reasoning is simple, if one is to invest adequate time in building up the land, he or she cannot spend an inordinate amount of time preoccupied for and tending to their personal safety. This is why war, far from being an economic boon, is ultimately fatal to man's efforts to build up the land.

How, then, can peace on earth be encouraged? The shockingly simple answer is that peace on earth can be achieved by allowing for uninhibited trade between communist style communities, such as families or tribes. As we explored in the previous chapter, the link between free trade and peace is so strong that it can be said that if goods do not cross borders, soldiers will. It may also be said that every

TO BUILD UP THE LAND: THOUGHTS ON MANKIND'S UNEASY INTERCOURSE WITH NATURE

form of taxation and custom or tariff charge imposed on goods and services in a geographical area serves to create fertile ground for social unrest due to the inevitable relative poverty in which the inhabitants of that territory will live.

It is on this fertile ground that the seeds of war are too often sown.

On the other hand, the mere removal of unnatural barriers to the free movement of goods and people, like the ones erected under the banner of taxation and tariffs, will serve to increase the relative prosperity of the land's inhabitants. This prosperity will encourage them to see their fate not as one that plays out in isolation and fear, but as a part of the greater human experience.

In this sense, free trade and the absence of taxation is the most effective form of defense known to man.

It all seems ideal, doesn't it? Living in peace, in perfect balance with nature and our fellow man. It doesn't sound like much to ask of everyone. Yet in practice, building up the land is a difficult endeavor. It is so difficult, that most people, when given the choice between working to build up the land and enjoying the fruits of the land, naturally choose the latter. The debt based money supply has allowed an unprecedented number of humans to spend more of their time enjoying the fruits of the land, and every day that this situation persists brings the actions of mankind further out of balance with the land's need to be built up.

The debt-based money supply not only serves to disconnect the monetary premium from the natural realm, it creates a completely unnatural and covert form of indentured servitude under which an ever-increasing portion of humanity finds itself. This type of covert servitude is perhaps more devastating to honest attempts to build up the land today than the sum of all imposed taxation and tariffs referred to above.

THE MYTH OF OVERPOPULATION

It is common in modern day urban environments to lament the lack of open spaces. Living in structures that are surrounded by other structures and spending time on overcrowded streets or public transportation systems tends to solidify the perception that there are too many people in one's immediate environment. The feeling is completely normal and understandable. What is not normal is to wish evil or impose limitations on others because of this perception, for a sober look at the data suggests that, while one's immediate surroundings may appear to be hopelessly overpopulated, the earth continues to suffer from chronic under population, or a lack of people willing to build up the land, in the parlance of Old Jules.

The answer, then, to a personal state of dissatisfaction with a perceived state of local overpopulation is to remove oneself from the overpopulated environment and relocate to a lower density locale.

There is no doubt that the world today is more densely populated than at any other time in its brief history. There is also no doubt that increasingly, mankind struggles to adequately nourish itself. It is an error, however, to blindly assume that an increased population is the root cause of relative shortages of food and potable water. It is equally erroneous to assume that there are limits to what the land can produce.

In Old Jules' day, the Sandhills of Northwestern Nebraska were harsh and relatively uninhabited. Old Jules recognized this as a problem. Untamed land is largely unproductive land. The land requires men and women to interact with it so that it will produce fruit and, in turn, allow the men and women to produce their own fruit, and so on.

Old Jules, like many inhabitants of what Nabokov called the "*Rotting old world*," or Europe, had come to America either in pursuit of greater opportunities or in flight from what amounted to a decrease of opportunities in Europe. This phenomenon was most notable in England, as the Industrial Revolution brought about an exponential improvement in general living conditions and life expectancies, it also brought a population boom which overwhelmed the natural boundries of the British Isles. It was there that the idea of overpopulation bloomed.

As war seemed to grip Europe from time to time, labor that would have otherwise been directed towards agricultural production was spent instead on the battlefield. Sadly, many of the men thrown into harm's way would not return, and agricultural production shortages were felt throughout the

TO BUILD UP THE LAND: THOUGHTS ON MANKIND'S UNEASY INTERCOURSE WITH NATURE

continent.

While most recognize the tragedy of war and the resulting misallocations of productive resources as avoidable, to some it may have seemed that the continent was beginning to suffer from overpopulation in the post war years. However, this feeling had nothing to do with actual scarcity of land. It was, rather, a result of the various wars, socialist policies, and other acts of aggression which hindered man's ability to build up the European soil to its full potential after the war had ended.

Such was the feeling of overpopulation during the 1800's and continuing, in many respects, through today, that people have left the war ravaged areas of Europe, creating perhaps the greatest wave of immigration that man has ever known to both the Northern and Southern Hemispheres of the Americas.

The land in the the middle of the North American continent was harsh and virgin. Yet, with a bit of luck and help from neighbors such as Old Jules, those who braved the frontier found an abundance of both resources and freedom beyond their wildest dreams.

What may come as a surprise is that this untamed frontier produced not a chaos of fiefdoms waging war against one another, but rather gave birth to perhaps the most honest and upstanding society that exists on the face of the earth. It is a society largely untainted by the banes of urban existence. It is a society that understands that the planet, far from having an overpopulation problem, suffers from a lack of people willing to roll up their sleeves and build up the land.

To encourage and help people to choose to build up the land has proven difficult, especially in the aftermath of the farm crisis of the 1970s and 80s in America. The crisis, which was largely the result of the sinkhole left in the money supply by erratic Federal Reserve policy, left thousands of family farms in ruin.

Even in Old Jules' day, it was difficult to find enough people willing to roll up their sleeves to build up the land. It required someone who had a vision for the land and could see past the allure of temporary personal gain so that both the people and the land could carry on their productive intercourse.

Again, we pick up with Mari Sandoz in Old Jules. This time, Sandoz describes Jules' efforts to assist homesteaders to take advantage of the Kinkaid Act of 1904, an amendment to the original Homesteaders act passed in the 1860's. Jules had hoped that the act would reign in the cattlemen and bring in the people that the land so desperately needed to build it up:

*"In the evening Jules, rifle across his arm, limped about among the newcomers and felt young again. It was like Valentine {**Nebraska}** in the eighties, but different too – many more people and not so young, not nearly so young Many of these were old – defeated men...*

"The day of the opening long queues of homeseekers waited for hours, only to find that even the sad choice of land that was free had been filed earlier in the day. There was talk of cattleman agents who made up baskets full of filing papers beforehand and ran them through the first thing. One woman

TO BUILD UP THE LAND: THOUGHTS ON MANKIND'S UNEASY INTERCOURSE WITH NATURE

was said to have filed on forty sections, under forty names, at five dollars a shot. The land was covered by filings that would never turn into farms. Yes, the Kinkaid Act as a cattleman law, as it was intended to be...

"Nevertheless Jules was busy. His buckskin team, colts of Old Daisy, threaded in and out between the hills. In six months, all unoccupied filings would be subject to contest. For twenty-five dollars Jules showed the land, ascertained the numbers, took the settler to Alliance to the land office, helped him make his filings, and later, when he was ready to fence, surveyed the homestead completely. If the homeseeker found nothing to please him, there was no charge. Otherwise, Jules pocketed the twenty-five dollar fee...

"And every few days some land agent or attorney from, say, Chicago suggested that Jules charge fifty or a hundred dollars and give him a fourth or half of the fee for steering prospects to him. Jules stuck his cob pipe between his bearded lips and threw the letters into the wood box.

"I am not in this business for the money. I'm trying to build up the country."

- Excerpts from "Old Jules" by Mari Sandoz

At the end of this discourse, Old Jules pins down the crux of the matter. If one is in pursuit of money, overpopulation will always be a problem. Money, as the good of highest order, is indirectly sought by all, and each additional person on the planet represents another competitor. This is an inescapable fact of the trappings of the debt based money supply in use today.

However, if one's aim is to build up the land, as was the case with Old Jules, they will quickly see that the truth of the matter, which the failure of the debt based money supply, as do all socialist machinations, serve to mask, is that money really does grow on well tended trees, and what is truly lacking are men and women brave enough to perform their conjugal duty to the land.

For without it, both the land and mankind will grow frigid, and the earth will become a cold and desolate place indeed.

A HARD OR GENTLE PEOPLE?

What type of person chooses to build up the land? In gentle climates, like the one we currently enjoy in the river valleys of Northwestern Oregon, where a minimal effort in planning and planting can often lead to an above average yield, gentle persons can build up the land. As the land is strong, the people don't have to be.

This has been true of the indigenous groups who inhabited the territories and, at the risk of offending our fellow Portlanders; we dare say that it is true of the population today. If one can stand the rain, life is relatively easy. A gentle, forgiving land will produce a gentle and forgiving people.

The corollary to this, naturally, is that a hard and unforgiving land will yield a hard and unforgiving people.

Again for proof of this, we turn to Mari Sandoz's account of her father, Old Jules. Jules Sandoz, our settler of 100 years ago, lived in a harsh land. He lived peacefully with the indigenous peoples there, who were being forced away by the Federal Army. He lived less peacefully with the bankers and cattlemen, who attempted to claim the land he was trying to build up by force.

In her account of his life, Mari Sandoz gives us a glimpse into her rough, determined, and surprisingly refined father:

"Jules Sandoz was not a nice man, but he was smart and tough and talented, and he was a survivor."

"Old Jules was always read to serve as a "locator," to help a new arrival stake out a claim and "find his corners," locate the precise boundaries of his land. For this, he charged little or nothing, as he wanted so badly to "build up, build up" the community."

"His (Old Jules') house was briefly the local post office, until he feuded with the officials and they took it away. His place was the unofficial storytelling center of the community. His skinny daughter, Marie (later Mari {the author}), would hang back in the darkness to stay up and listen to the immigrants and Indians {Indigenous peoples} and, less frequently, the cowboys tell their tales.

Old Jules maintained a well-stocked medical kit and was the unofficial frontier doctor to one and all. He befriended the local Indians, some of the last Lakotas to live free in lodges, tipis, near his home. They called him "Straight Eye," honoring his shooting skill. He spent windfall money he could ill afford on a Victrola {record player} and phonograph records, because he liked good music and thought he and his family should have it. They loved it."

"Old Jules became a nationally known fruit breeder and grower, a correspondent of Luther Burbank. He

TO BUILD UP THE LAND: THOUGHTS ON MANKIND'S UNEASY INTERCOURSE WITH NATURE

was sure that this land was ideal for raising cherries. He was wrong. It wasn't.

- Excerpts from "Old Jules" by Mari Sandoz

It took hard people, like Old Jules and the nomadic indigenous peoples who passed through the Sandhills following the bison, to slowly build up a hard land. As the land became softer, Old Jules became softer. For this reason, Old Jules was passionate about bringing settlers to the Sandhills to build up the land.

Today, the Sandhills of Western Nebraska are inhabited by kinder persons who have reaped the benefits of the efforts of pioneers like Old Jules. He and countless others whom he encouraged have worked to build up the land to a point where the effort to build it up is falling into balance with the time spent enjoying its fruits.

In Oregon and the Pacific Northwest, the opposite may be happening. Attempts to minimize man's interaction with the land via conservation, essentially declaring the land off limits for development, are returning countless acres of land to a state of wilderness. While the efforts are noble and well intentioned, this too will, over time, throw the efforts of man to build up the land out of balance with the time spend enjoying the fruits of the land.

For it is true that the land needs rest, just as man needs rest. But rest must come in the right proportion for both man and the land to maintain their edge and to keep the dynamic between mankind and the land in a healthy balance, allowing both to rest and produce in a perfect proportion, providing for the future without robbing the next generation of the tools needed to continue building it up.

THE LAND NEEDS REST

There is indeed in nature a perfect balance between the time for building up the land and that for allowing the land to rest. This balance of time is commonly known as the Sabbath, it is a pattern of time that has literally been encoded into the creation itself.

The Sabbath is best known, at least in the United States, as a weekly Jewish religious observance. The base of the observance is taken from two passages in the Torah:

2 On the seventh day God finished his work which he had done; and he rested on the seventh day from all his work which he had done. 3 God blessed the seventh day, and made it holy, because he rested in it from all his work of creation which he had done.

- Genesis 2:2-3

12 "Observe the Sabbath day, to keep it holy, as

Yahweh your God commanded you. 13 You shall labor six days, and do all your work; 14 but the seventh day is a Sabbath to Yahweh your God, in which you shall not do any work, you, nor your son, nor your daughter, nor your male servant, nor your female servant, nor your ox, nor your donkey, nor any of your livestock, nor your stranger who is within your gates; that your male servant and your female servant may rest as well as you. 15 You shall remember that you were a servant in the land of Egypt, and Yahweh your God brought you out of there by a mighty hand and by an outstretched arm. Therefore Yahweh your God commanded you to keep the Sabbath day.

- Deuteronomy 5:12-15

The seven day weekly cycle that is anchored by the Sabbath is so entrenched in the creation that every attempt by man to supersede it, the most notable recent attempts being the French Republican Calendar and the Soviet Calendar. Both were suspended after experiments that lasted roughly twelve years.

While the texts in the Torah, which form part of the Christian Bible, offer clear guidance by the divine to observe not only a seven day week, but a seven day week consisting of six days of work and one day of rest, religious tradition alone cannot account for the origins of the seven day cycle.

Cultures throughout the world have operated on weekly structures consisting of anywhere between three and thirteen days, notable ancient examples are the eight-day Roman market calendar and the 13-day Mayan week. Indeed, it appears that the Jews did not widely observe the seventh day Sabbath until they were exiled to Babylonian captivity between 597 and 587 BCE.

Adding to the mystery of the seven-day week is that it is they only time construct known to mankind that does not conform to any astrological, lunar, or solar cycle, as days, months, and years are designed to do.

Dr. Franz Halberg at the University of Minnesota is the foremost authority on natural rhythms, which are the subject matter of an area of science known as chronobiology. Through nearly 70 years of research, Halberg has discovered that all rhythmic functions of the human body are likely to possess an innate seven-day frequency.

The findings of Dr. Halberg's research suggests that the primary reason that the seven-day weekly cycle has emerged as the dominant time cycle that is now observed by every large society on the planet is by virtue of the fact that seven-day cycles are deeply ingrained in human, plant, and animal life at a cellular level. The divine call for a day of rest every seventh day appears to fit perfectly with an unseen but deeply felt rhythm common to the interplay between all living things down to the most basic cellular level.

While an understanding of the seven day weekly cycle and the need to collectively rest on the seventh day is somewhat easy to grasp based on personal experience for most, what is harder to grasp but equally and perhaps more important with regards to building up the land is the need for the land to rest every seventh year.

In other words, the seemingly arbitrary command

to abstain from work on the seventh day not only applies to the cycle of days known as the week, but the need to rest on the seventh year of a cycle after six years of production as well.

Again, the basis for the resting of the land on the seventh year by abstaining from all productive agricultural activity upon it can be found in the Torah:

10 "For six years you shall sow your land, and shall gather in its increase, 11 but the seventh year you shall let it rest and lie fallow, that the poor of your people may eat; and what they leave the animal of the field shall eat. In the same way, you shall deal with your vineyard and with your olive grove.

- Exodus 23:10-11

2 "Speak to the children of Israel, and tell them, 'When you come into the land which I give you, then the land shall keep a Sabbath to Yahweh. 3 You shall sow your field six years, and you shall prune your vineyard six years, and gather in its fruits; 4 but in the seventh year there shall be a Sabbath of solemn rest for the land, a Sabbath to Yahweh. You shall not sow your field or prune your vineyard. 5 What grows of itself in your harvest you shall not reap, and you shall not gather the grapes of your undressed vine. It shall be a year of solemn rest for the land. 6 The Sabbath of the land shall be for food for you; for yourself, for your servant, for your maid, for your hired servant, and for your stranger, who lives as a foreigner with you. 7 For your livestock also, and for the animals that are in your land, shall all its increase be for food.

TO BUILD UP THE LAND: THOUGHTS ON MANKIND'S UNEASY INTERCOURSE WITH NATURE

- Leviticus 25:2-7

The command to rest the land every seventh year is often embodied in a practice that is known as crop rotation. Crop rotation is a method of agriculture in which a series of different types of crops are planted in the same area, usually a field, in sequential growing seasons.

The planting of different seeds on the same field each season helps the land to achieve balance because different types of plants require of and provide to the land different types of nutrients, allowing the land to replenish itself. An additional benefit to crop rotation can be found with relation to pests. By constantly changing the types of crops grown in a certain area, the farmer can avoid the possibility that a pest would become entrenched in an area, as simply changing crops can deprive certain pests of the means necessary to establish viable habitats over long periods of time for their colonies.

Many crop rotation plans call for a field to lie fallow for a season. While the benefits of allowing the land to rest are numerous, the most common benefit of this practice is that it allows the water table underneath the Land to reestablish itself in anticipation of providing crops for the next six years. Given that water tables are not field specific, but cover large areas encompassing many fields, it is important that the fallow years for fields be coordinated to coincide with each other for the benefits of the Sabbath year to accrue to the land and, consequently, to the land's inhabitants.

THE MODERN CHALLENGE OF COORDINATED REST

While the concept of rest is widely understood and practiced, both human and agricultural observances of the Sabbath in the modern world tend to suffer from a lack of coordination. While diversity in Sabbath observances is normal and beneficial over long distances, localized diversity in these observances, while at first appearing to have many clear benefits, are ultimately detrimental to the intent of the Sabbath, which is to draw the activities of mankind into harmony and balance with both the Land and each other.

The decoupling of the monetary premium from the natural realm is the primary contributor to the lack of coordination among the natural resting periods called for by the rhythm of life at both a cellular and integrated systems level.

While the ideas of mankind are boundless, the time and resources required to realize them are not. When the monetary premium is fixed in the natural realm, mankind's creative energy and resulting activities are more likely to be in harmony with both nature and the activities of one another.

However, as the monetary premium today primarily rests on an interest bearing credit instrument, the demand for repayment with interest places an extraordinary burden on both mankind and, by extension, the land.

*{**Editor's Note**: A fine refutation of usury, which is beyond the scope of this volume, may be found at Jason Hommel's Silver Stock Report}*

As a consequence, mankind's activities, which are more often than not directed at satisfying the demands of these credit instruments, do not allow for adequate periods of rest, much less rest in a coordinated fashion. This lack of coordinated rest has significantly contributed the imbalances in the world today.

Paradoxically, it is mankind's lack of individual and coordinated rest that is the biggest obstacle to his efforts to build up the land. For the land will build itself up on its own, if we would just leave it be one of every seven years. If the land is not allowed to rest on this divinely designed interval, it will eventually capitulate due to lack of nutrients and take its rest all at once, no matter how much seed or fertilizer is applied to it.

Both mankind and the land must partake in their naturally mandated rest for the rhythm of life on earth to achieve balance. This rest is most effective if it is taken in a coordinated manner, meaning that mankind rests on every seventh day, in unison with those around him, and that the land be allowed to rest every seventh year, again, in unison with the land around it.

The onus of observing the natural cycles of rest falls squarely upon the shoulders of mankind. Observance of the Sabbaths requires a level of collective self-control that few individuals, let alone societies, possess. Will we return to them before it is too late?

CONSERVATION, WHAT OCCURS WHEN MAN ATTEMPTS TO CONTROL RATHER THAN BUILD UP THE LAND

The concept of the Sabbath rest is a concrete example of both the codependence of man upon the land, and the land upon man to build it up and give it rest. While the former statement is obvious, what may be less clear in light of today's political and environmental climate is the latter.

Does the land really need man to tend to it so that it, too, will prosper? The clear answer is that the land not only needs the activity of man upon it to survive and thrive, but also that of animals. However, the land does not simply need human activity, it requires coordinated human activity in order to achieve balance.

Today, there are roughly 7.1 billion souls on the planet, more than at any other time in human history. If one watches the numbers roll on the page linked above and then sees that the world's net population is on track to grow by roughly 80 million souls this year alone, it would appear that this population grow is nothing short of exponential and that the world's population is on something akin to a warp curve when plotted out graphically.

However, while 80 million souls per year seems a staggering amount, it is important to note that the actual growth rate, as a percentage of the current population, is on a gentle decline, currently at 1.1%, which is just half the growth rate experienced in the early 1960's, the most recent peak based on projections by the United Nations. The United Nations further anticipates that by 2050, the growth rate will again be halved to just 0.5%, and that the world's population will stabilize at around 10 billion persons after 2100.

As we have explored earlier, overpopulation is largely a myth constructed by persons who both live in crowded urban areas and assume that current statistical trends will invariably play out.

The myth is intensified by the fact that a majority of mankind has chosen to live in urban settings and has left large swaths of land to lie fallow, something that ultimately benefits neither man nor the land. According to statistics in the 2013 edition of Demographia's report on World Urban Areas, roughly three out of every ten persons, or 28.2% of the world's population, lives in an urban area of over 500,000 total inhabitants with an average density of 14,000 persons per square mile.

The current increase in urban populations and corresponding worldview has left an increasing burden on those who have remained to build up the land via agriculture to provide the food necessary for

TO BUILD UP THE LAND: THOUGHTS ON MANKIND'S UNEASY INTERCOURSE WITH NATURE

the 7.1 billion (and counting) living souls to survive and be adequately nourished.

If one, For the sake of argument, were to make the broad assumption that those living in urban areas were completely reliant on their rural counterparts for their food supply in an equal proportion, this would mean that the rural population must produce, on average, 139.3% of their annual food consumption. In other words, they must produce enough food for both 100% of their own consumption and an additional 39.3% to be consumed by the otherwise occupied urbanites.

However, this is an overly simplified view of the actual dynamics of food production, for while a small proportion of urbanites may collectively achieve communal or territorial self-sufficiency when it comes to food production, an overwhelming percentage of urbanites are not in a position to do this and, as such, are fully reliant upon their rural counterparts. Conversely, not all persons living in rural communities are dedicated to agriculture.

What, then, is the true ratio? How many persons are dedicated to building up the land?

It is a fact that, on average, each American farmer produces enough food to feed 155 people. This is up from roughly 26 people in 1960 and in statistical terms means that one person armed with the proper agricultural equipment and technology and favorable climate patterns can produce 15,500% of their own caloric requirements.

This staggering advance in American agricultural productivity is largely owing to the extended period of peace that has reigned in America, which gave birth to, or at a minimum coincided with rapid advances in agricultural science and industrial machinery.

It may be said, then, that these advances in agriculture have made possible the urban centric worldview that is widely espoused today. This is not a bad thing, however, and the current awareness of climate change and its potential impact on the increasingly delicate food chain upon which an increasing majority of the world depends is rightly cause for alarm.

However, this alarm has lead to an obsession with both conservation policies and excessive regulations on agricultural activities. This obsession, if left unchecked, will further isolate mankind from the land, and places unnecessary burdens upon those who are building up the land.

If mankind's intercourse with the land is restricted through conservation to the point of sterility, the delicate food chain, which such policies and regulations seek to protect, will collapse.

AGRICULTURAL ALARMS: GMOS AND CAFOS

While the fact that one American farmer can provide nourishment for up to 155 persons is a staggering testament to advances in agricultural methods and technology, these advances have been aided by the two developments, one in seed production and the other in animal husbandry, that have given rise to controversy regarding their long term affects on both the land and mankind.

These developments, Genetically Modified Organisms, or GMOs, and Confined Animal Feeding Operations, or CAFOs, have found themselves at the heart of debates surrounding the cause of both health issues in humans as well as the phenomenon of climate change. The level of animosity which opposition to these developments often rises is extraordinary, and the stakes could not be higher.

On one side, proponents of GMOs and CAFOs hold that production of food on the scale that these developments allow could not be achieved via other means, and that literally billions of human lives would not even be possible save for the increase in food production made possible by their employment.

On the other, opponents of GMOs and CAFOs hold that these developments rely upon unnatural alterations of the base of the food chain that will ultimately manifest themselves in poorer overall public health and, in the worst case scenario, threatens to severely disrupt the food supply through any number of unforeseen risks of failure that are inherently embedded in these methods of agriculture and animal husbandry that are now practiced on a very large scale.

Given the high stakes involved on both sides of the debate, we have coined the term "Agricultural Alarms" to encompass the dual opportunity and threat presented by the widespread use of GMOs in agriculture and CAFOs in the production of animal based food products.

GENETICALLY MODIFIED ORGANISMS (GMOS)

The question that is at the heart of the present debate on the merits of using Genetically Modified Organisms in seeds and the modified seeds' reliance upon pesticides to ensure adequate crop yields is the following: At what long term cost does this productivity come?

It is an important question, for the long-term security of the world's food supply may hang in the balance.

Genetically Modified Organisms, or GMOs, are a prime example of mankind's attempt to control nature. It is a form of conservation in that it attempts to conserve the current balance of food production by creating crop yields in excess of that which would occur under normal conditions.

It cannot be argued that GMOs have played a major role in human population growth. However, it is also clear that there are many potential and actual direct and indirect side effects to exerting this type of control over the food chain that have yet to fully manifest themselves.

First and foremost, the staggering crop yields that the combination of GMO seeds, fertilizer, and pesticides make possible come at a high price for the land itself. Rather than achieving a balance with the land, allowing it to produce and rest in natural occurring intervals with intermittent obligatory rests in the form of Sabbath years for agricultural land and herd rotations for pasturelands, mankind's GMO induced yield highs serve to convert the land into an addict, unable to function without increasingly regular shots of fertilizer and irrigation.

Again, fertilization and irrigation are important parts of farming and the building up of agricultural land when done in moderation. However, when these tasks are taken to extremes, they rob both the land and mankind of their most important survival mechanism: Self-sufficiency.

ARE GMOS A FORM OF PRIVATE PROPERTY OR POLLUTION?

On the surface, GMOs appear to be nothing more than a benign attempt to increase yields by creating crops that are resistant to pests and blight. However, far beyond the documented health and biodiversity concerns that are often associated with GMOs, we see that GMOs may, by virtue of their resilience, unwittingly violate the private property of others.

While simple labeling requirements, which in theory would give consumers the power to choose whether or not to purchase GMO tainted foods, would satisfy most consumers health fears, there are large scale problems with respect to the reach of patent law as well as biodiversity concerns with GMOs that rise to a level that should concern all of humanity.

The root of the problem is the legal argument that the genetic codes developed for use in the creation of GMOs are the property of the creator of that code. In practice, this legal argument does not limit ownership of the code to seeds that the creator has physically produced, but to any seed or resulting crop that is found to contain the genetic code, regardless of origin. As such, once a GMO crop is planted, nature's natural cross pollinators, namely wind and bees, will carry the genetic code to crops in surrounding fields, making the crops in those fields technically the property of the creator of the genetic code.

Under current law, once a neighboring crop has become tainted with the genetic code that has been transferred to it via natural means, the code creator can demand remuneration from the farmer or grower of the previously untainted crop for use of the genetic code, even though the use was incidental.

This current legal interpretation of GMO patents is perhaps the most insidious example of Empire, whose ultimate goal is to be in a position to demand the food production of a population and force that same population to come begging it for the same food stuffs that the people had produced and rendered as tribute.

Generally, the courts have ruled in favor of the GMO genetic code creators at the expense of farmers who do not use GMO seed and, by extension, all of humanity. In the process the justices, who are under the impression that they are upholding private property by virtue of their rulings, are in practice destroying it.

There is an inherent conflict between intellectual property and tangible property. As long as intellectual property rights are allowed to trample tangible property rights, all of humanity will suffer and become further enslaved.

The situation, seen through a different lens, would have a different outcome if the farmer or grower who was being sued by a GMO producer would begin to mount defenses based on tangible property rights, for in practice what is occurring is that the products of the GMO creators are indirectly polluting the private property of the non GMO farmers.

The arguments for the GMO creators generally hinge on the fact that neighboring farmers have enjoyed greater yields by virtue of their "enhancements." If the battle over imposed intellectual property is to be won, farmers must reject the increased yield arguments by presenting the argument that their crops have not been enhanced, but tainted by the spread of GMO through natural pollination processes, which know no boundary lines. The legal issue must be argued as a question of quality, not quantity.

The involuntary spread of GMO genetic code to neighboring crops is pollution. Until the farmers and justices begin to see it as such, the natural biodiversity of the world's food supply, which is its true protector from pests, drought, and blight, will continue to suffer harm and a heightened risk of collapse.

CONFINED ANIMAL FEEDING OPERATIONS (CAFOS)

Another perhaps less known but equally widespread practice that may ultimately threaten the food supply is the food industry's increased reliance upon Confined Animal Feeding Operations, or CAFOs.

The proliferation of CAFOs, which are facilities where animals are raised in relatively cramped quarters, fed things that are not part of their natural diet (the equivalent of fertilizer in the GMO example above), and injected with antibiotics (the equivalent of pesticides in the above example) pose a twofold threat to the environment.

First, it produces animal based foodstuffs that have been proven to be harmful to humans over time. Second, and perhaps more importantly for reasons that are obvious, it limits the animals' natural and mutually beneficial interaction with the land which robs the land of an important means of natural fertilization and rejuvenation, urine and manure.

TO BUILD UP THE LAND: THOUGHTS ON MANKIND'S UNEASY INTERCOURSE WITH NATURE

After a personal epiphany regarding the detriments of setting apart land for conservation, a practice that is widely thought to be beneficial, Ecologist Allan Savory has made it his life's work to reverse what he now sees as a dangerous policy of land conservation being pursued by environmental activists and governmental land management groups around the globe.

For over a century, well meaning ecologists like Mr. Savory have labored under the belief that desertification, the fate that awaits the land when mankind and animals cease or severely limit their intercourse with it, was the direct result of large herds of animals grazing upon the land.

The initial conclusion of attributing desertification to large scale animal grazing is a logical one. After all, if one has seen the relative devastation that large herds leave in their wake as they move across a field, one can only conclude that the animals alone are responsible for desertification, as they leave the land barren and trampled.

Yet Savory holds out that this first analysis is incomplete. In fact, it is necessary for animals to consume, trample on, and leave their excretions on the land so that it may be left in peace to rejuvenate itself with the necessary fertilizer and just the amount of greenery necessary to thrive.

Part of the logic of Mr. Savory's approach is that if the animals are left to graze freely, they will leave the land for greener pastures, as it were, once they have eaten the top layers of grass and shrubbery, the equivalent of pruning a plant. Furthermore, the animals will quickly tire, as anyone would, of tromping through their own excrements in search of food, leaving the land both pruned and fertilized. The land will then be left rejuvenate itself in time for the next grazing cycle.

While it has long remained on the fringe of land management, Mr. Savory's work has received the endorsement of royalty. At the 2012 World Conservation Congress, none other than the Prince of Wales gave this glowing endorsement of Savory's methods:

"I have been particularly fascinated, for example, by the work of a remarkable man called Allan Savory, in Zimbabwe and other semiarid areas, who has argued for years against the prevailing expert view that it is the simple numbers of cattle that drive overgrazing and cause fertile land to become desert. On the contrary, as he has since shown so graphically, the land needs the presence of feeding animals and their droppings for the cycle to be complete, so that soils and grassland areas stay productive. Such that, if you take grazers off the land and lock them away in vast feedlots, the land dies."

- *2012 Quote by Charles, Prince of Wales {via wikipedia.org}*

While GMOs and CAFOs may appear to be nothing short of modern miracles with respect to increasing the global food supply, they are a direct result of man attempting to control the land as opposed to working with the land for mutual benefit.

Left to its own devices, mankind will destroy the land to the extent that it wishes to unilaterally exert its will upon it. What is needed, then, is an acute awareness that to destroy the land through an exertion of unnatural control over it, the type of control that is the logical end of the philosophies that have given rise to GMOs and CAFOs, is to destroy ourselves.

CONSERVATION DOOMS THE LAND TO DESERTIFICATION

It is clear that the land, mankind, and animals live together in a delicate balance. Maintenance of this balance requires both constant interaction between mankind and nature and a measure of restraint. This restraint can only begin with a general acknowledgement that nature cannot be completely controlled in a healthy manner.

The opposite of the action of building up the land is a term that implies something that could not be farther from the truth: Conservation.

The term conservation implies the maintenance and upkeep of something. In terms of land management, it may be mistaken for actions taken or not taken to build up the land. However, in practice, conservation has come to embody a form of forced abstinence on the part of man with regards to the land.

There is much debate and scientific evidence which points to the activities of mankind being the

TO BUILD UP THE LAND: THOUGHTS ON MANKIND'S UNEASY INTERCOURSE WITH NATURE

ultimate cause of climate change and desertification. These findings are true to the extent that mankind's activities are not aimed at building up the land. However, the only thing worse than mankind working to throw nature further out of balance by chasing a misplaced monetary premium roughshod over it is for mankind to abstain from interacting with the land altogether in a vain hope that the land would be better of without us.

The land needs mankind, and mankind needs the land. Both the land and mankind need animals to freely roam over the land rather than suffer in the constraints of a CAFO, the equivalent of prison in the animal world. All efforts to halt these natural interactions are an unwitting step towards squandering what arable land remains on the planet.

The problem lies not in mankind's interaction with the land, rather, it lies in the attribution of the monetary premium, which often is the ultimate guide of human actions, to debt instruments, which do not originate in the natural world, but in the unbridled imaginations of men and women.

When properly placed in the natural world, the monetary premium guides mankind's actions in concert with the needs of the land, the ultimate effect being that the land is built up. When the monetary premium is anchored to nothing more than human fancies, mankind's actions are invariably separated from the needs of the land, leaving the burden on the land itself to conform to these whims.

Like all conjugal relationships where one party acts unilaterally, it will end in disaster. However, mankind cannot be divorced from the land, for ours is an eternal connection, and the incessant abuse of the land by mankind threatens to destroy both parties.

For this reason alone, mankind must recognize that the monetary premium must be primarily attributed to things in the natural realm. If it is not, our every pursuit will serve to devour us.

WHY THE MONETARY PREMIUM MUST BE ATTRIBUTED TO A TANGIBLE GOOD

While the issue of climate change has largely been settled, the raging debate over climate change has moved to the sphere of identifying its root cause or causes. Be it carbon emissions or over-grazing, the common mantra throughout this shared experience has been, *"mankind has caused this problem, and mankind can fix it."*

Unfortunately, "fixing" climate change often takes the form of violently raging against Genetically Modified crops, faceless agricultural and petroleum related corporate interests, and a host of conspiracy theories too long to even begin to count.

It is unfortunate because climate change has just one root cause that mankind has consistently and perhaps willfully overlooked: The attribution of the monetary premium primarily to debt instruments.

What we have alluded to in earlier chapters, we

will now lay out plainly, for it is our underlying premise and our ultimate contribution to man's understanding of monetary theory: The monetary premium, which is the increase in the value of an object owed to its usefulness as a store of value, medium of exchange, and/or unit of account, must be primarily attached to a tangible good for the activities which mankind carries out to be in balance with the resources that exist in natural world.

The world has operated on a system of fiat currency, or currency by decree, on and off for as long as there has been an Empire capable of dictating what its subjects must use as money in settlement of debts. Fiat currency is not harmful in and of itself. In fact, given enough time, any fiat currency which is not flexible enough to change with the needs of the economic activity which it is intended to aid will either self destruct on its own, owed to it being eschewed in favor of a more suitable currency, or, if its use is rigidly enforced, cause the underlying economic activity to self destruct or cease, causing another form of fiat collapse.

To control what is used as money and the monetary premium represents the ultimate power in the material world. As such, such control can never be gained by force. Rather, it must be created by a great many deceptions which cause otherwise rational persons to hand over control over this most important of decisions.

For over 40 years now, much of the world has not only subjugated itself to accepting a form of fiat in exchange for the fruit of their labors, it has come to accept as money the worst form of fiat, a fiat currency that comes into being as a debt instrument. As a result, mankind has tacitly attributed this precious monetary premium to credit, which is not dependent upon the production of goods in the real world, nor on existing property, rather, it is primarily dependent upon the character of man.

The following quotations speak directly to this often unspoken but most important detail with regards to the nature of credit:

"Credit is not money. Credit is trust. Trust can vanish in an instant."

- Frederick J. Sheehan, March 25, 2013

In response to questioning by Samuel Untermeyer during the Pujo Committee hearings, J.P. Morgan famously made the following observations on money and credit *{**Editor's note:** You may read the Pujo Committee, formally known as the Money Trust Investigation, testimonies via the St. Louis Fed}:*

*"**Untermyer:** 'The basis of banking is credit, is it not?"*

*"**Morgan:** "Not always. That is evidence of banking, but it is not the money itself. Money is gold, and nothing else."*

Then, during the same lime of testimony:

*"**Untermyer:** "Is not commercial credit based*

primarily on money or property?

Morgan: *"No sir, the first thing is character.*

Untermyer: *"Before money or property?*

Morgan: *"Before money or property or anything else. Money cannot buy it"*

Both Sheehan and Morgan's observations on credit are sufficient to gain an understanding of what credit, and by extension today's monetary premium, really is.

Most persons are conditioned to assume that credit is backed by collateral. However, were credit backed by collateral, it would cease to be credit. The essence of credit is trust. Trust, by definition, is created by the belief in an inherently uncertain future outcome. It would follow, then, that trust might not always be well placed. The plans upon which the credit and underlying trust are built may just as easily not turn out as planned as they would turn out according to plan.

Money, the basis of banking, cannot be destroyed, it can only change hands. Credit and trust, however, can be destroyed in an instant, for they are subject to the fickle decisions and imperfect plans of men.

When money is based on trust as opposed to something that is indestructible, the world moves to a very dangerous place with regards to the planning of daily activities. This is where the world is today, circa 2013, after 40 years of what we refer to as the "insane, debt is money," financial system.

TO BUILD UP THE LAND: THOUGHTS ON MANKIND'S UNEASY INTERCOURSE WITH NATURE

Trust is good and necessary to a point; however, it can vanish in an instant. When there is an excess amount of trust, or promises to pay, circulating in relationship to a finite number of money, goods, and capital in the real world, there are bound to be a few broken promises.

CONCLUSION

If kept to a minimum, the economic systems that are organically created by mankind to deal with scarcity via the conduct of trade, a collection of systems that we call True Capitalism, will correct the errors that result from misplaced trust that manifests itself in credits that are defaulted upon. The damage to the economic systems will be isolated and the activities of men will then be forced to return to balance with the underlying natural resources of the earth.

However, if misplaced trust in the form of bad credits are allowed to perpetuate themselves without a natural means by which to eliminate them, mankind will have no incentive to investigate whom amongst them is worthy of the trust that credit represents. This state of being will, and indeed does, cause much of the earth's natural resources to fall into unproductive hands where it will ultimately be squandered.

Meanwhile, those who are capable will not be able to coordinate their efforts with their fellow men in any meaningful way. Indeed, the ones who are capable will simply learn how to take advantage of the over abundance of trust which is being created rather than dedicate their efforts towards productive activities which require relatively greater sacrifices.

This dual proliferation and misallocation of trust has two real world consequences:

1. Natural resources are wasted at an alarming rate. For this reason the placement of the monetary premium on debt instruments, or credits, has lead to the crisis of Climate Change (otherwise known as Global Warming). This represents a myriad of symptoms whose root cause is that man's activities are severely out of balance with the demands of the natural world. The cause of this imbalance in the current situation is that man's activities, both those worthy of trust that have succeeded and those that have failed miserably, have been greatly accelerated by the high octane mix of credit and the monetary premium that circulates as currency in the economy.

Man is in a desperate race to meet a timetable that the earth's resources cannot provide for. The result is the severe imbalances that we now observe. It is this, and not the industrial revolution, fossil fuels, or any of the other symptoms that is the root cause of climate change.

2. While there are a great deal of men who are busy scorching the earth with their activities, the wise have learned to concentrate their efforts not on the productive activities to which they would otherwise dedicate themselves, but to profiting from the explosion of trust and credit, constantly maneuvering themselves into a position to profit from the misjudgments and miscalculations or their fellow men.

Beneath all of this misguided economic activity, the land itself is either being scorched or left to lie fallow rather than being built up as Old Jules encouraged.

However, it is not man himself or any of his inventions that constitute the root cause of the problem. Rather, it is the simple misplacement of the monetary premium on credit instruments which emits the false signals that all of mankind either follows or is forced to follow in the planning and execution of its daily activities.

Fortunately, the remedy for climate change is as simple as it sounds: Allow the monetary premium to return to the natural world.

Notice that the active verb above is *allow*, not force, legislate, or otherwise coerce. If our premise holds, then it would follow that the monetary premium would attach itself to things in the natural realm in a completely organic and fluid manner. There is nothing to be done at all; in fact, there are a great many things that should be left undone.

Above all, mankind must embrace freedom in all spheres of life, most importantly with regards to money and banking. Until this final frontier of freedom is reclaimed, both mankind and the land will suffer the consequences of a warped form of unilateral intercourse.

The battlefield for this final frontier of freedom is within our minds, for freedom from the shackles of a debt based monetary system must first be won on the realm of ideas for it to manifest itself in the activities and dealings of men, both with regards to the land as well as with one another, for both are desperately in need of being built up.

APPENDIX A: THE GREAT GREEN WALL, AND ARE YOU A SOLDIER, AN ATHLETE, OR A FARMER?

Whether one currently finds themselves living in an urban environment with little connection to the land or out in the fields, toiling daily to build it up, they are likely to find themselves identifying with one of three basic examples of behavior and motivations.

These examples were first presented to us in the summer of 2004 at a Kings Kids European summit in Tarragona. Far from the lush EU summits that are the hallmark of today's famous Troika mismanagement, the Kings Kids operate on a wing and, most literally, a prayer.

With our Castilian Spanish skills still lacking, we spent a mid summer's week in tents on a high school campus (naturally, school was out) with minimal bath and shower facilities along with hundreds of adolescents, young adults, and not so young adults from across Europe and the UK (indeed, we were acquainted with a long lost cousin from Wales at the event). It is in these settings where Yahweh moves and provides his most profound lessons and training.

It was in this setting that the examples referred to in the title of this appendix were presented by our Pastor Curtis Clewett of La Iglesia El Lokal in Barcelona. Each time we recount the impact of this teaching to him, he recalls it as something that he threw together at the last minute.

So it was, on a warm summers eve on the Mediterranean coast in a place which more or less resembled a gypsy camp, we gathered to hear el Reverendo impart the three examples of what we will call spiritual maturity. Read them carefully and please, take no offense to the blanket statements that the descriptions imply. We understand there are many shades of the following professions, and it will quickly become clear that it is the description that matters more than the professional title. Read the descriptions carefully and look for yourself in one of them, for how one identifies with the following professional examples will help them gain an understanding of how they will react in the constant chase of the elusive monetary premium:

The Soldier: The soldier is in training. He is fit, well equipped, and he is at the ready. However, the soldier does not represent the ultimate in spiritual maturity, for he is lacking two things: Initiative and autonomy.

The soldier is trained to take orders. He does not dare act on his own for fear of retribution or failure.

He is limited by not only the rules and regulations of his trade, but also in his physical movements and the ability to act independently of the orders given by his commanders. As such, he cannot act on his own initiative and, if he does, it is in a very small sphere of operations which is largely dependent upon others following similar orders.

Being a soldier is not a bad thing, indeed, it is admirable, but journey of spiritual growth demands that he move past this necessary first jaunt down the never-ending path towards spiritual maturity.

The Athlete: Unlike the soldier, the athlete is, by definition, acting on his or her own initiative. They may depend upon a coach for guidance and encouragement, but their motivation to obey the coach comes from a desire to improve, not fear, as was the case from time to time with the soldier.

The athlete desires to excel at a certain sport or event, and relies on set intervals of competitions or time trials by which to receive feedback and praise for his or her efforts.

Again, being an athlete is not a bad thing, and the emergence of personal initiative and the desire to train, as well as an increased degree of autonomy represent a further journey down the path to spiritual maturity, however, even if the athlete reaches the pinnacle of their chosen field, they are still lacking in one very important aspect, an aspect that is fully embraced by the farmer.

The Farmer: The farmer does not have a drill sergeant yelling at him in the morning, nor is he told what to do or when to do it. The farmer is rarely

TO BUILD UP THE LAND: THOUGHTS ON MANKIND'S UNEASY INTERCOURSE WITH NATURE

restricted in his movements or daily activities by anyone other than himself.

The farmer does not train on a daily basis and is not accountable to a coach. Indeed, the farmer takes on responsibility not only for his own training regimen, but also for understanding when and where to compete.

The farmer knows exactly what to do and waits for signals from his natural surroundings to tell him when to do it. He constantly looks after his surroundings and understands that both the land and the animals within his care have been entrusted to him. Indeed, so have his family and his neighbors. Even those whom he will never meet may indirectly rely upon the success of his efforts to be able to put food on their table.

The farmer's efforts may appear volatile, oscillating between sloth and frenzies of chaotic activity. When there is nothing to be done, the farmer drives to the café to drink coffee and play cards all day. When there is work to be done, he awakens early and does not rest until his equipment or the lack of daylight put an end to the day's efforts.

The farmer not only understands what needs to be done, he understands that all efforts, to be effective, must be put forth in their season. He can prepare, and often does, but he understands that the time to exert himself will become known in its due time, and it will not happen on a schedule that he can set.

Still, he accepts the responsibility of his post, both the long days and the stinging boredom, with joy, knowing that ultimately he is doing the work of a master, and is providing for many who live well beyond the county line who he may never personally meet. He may never be thanked by them or be recognized formally for his work, yet it is in the work itself that he finds life's greatest contentment.

As you can see from the above examples, to understand one's own character when interacting with the monetary premium, it is as important to understand who we are serving as it is to understand how we are serving, for the key to contentment lies in choosing well on both accounts.

The monetary premium currently attributed to debt and credit instruments represented by today's fiat currencies will take wings. If one is a soldier or an athlete, they are likely to get burned. However, the farmer, in a sloth like manner, will pick his spot and wait patiently for an opportunity to return the monetary premium to its rightful place in the land. When that opportunity appears, he will, in a sudden, measured frenzy, labor night and day until the work is finished.

Pastor Clewett is still in Barcelona. In the true spirit of the farmer, he continues to pastor in addition to his duties at Planting Together, where he is on the Executive team. Planting Together is an organization which organizes tree planting and pruning excursions, where they partner with the government of Senegal and many others to help build up the Great Green Wall, a wall of trees and foliage which is successfully fighting back the encroachment of the Sahara in northwestern Africa.

Eschatology & Money

A BRIEF LOOK AT WHAT IS TO COME

Epilogue

EPILOGUE: ESCHATOLOGY AND MONEY: A BRIEF LOOK AT WHAT IS TO COME

CONTENTS

Introduction	363
Give to Caesar What is Caesar's	366
The Vision of John	369
The Vision of Daniel	375
Conclusion and Encouragement	380

INTRODUCTION

Contemplating the end times as they are presented in the Bible can be daunting. Christians who accept the Bible as God's word vacillate somewhere between two extremes, either ignoring completely what is written or spending an inordinate amount of time and energy looking for signs that the prophecies are nearing fulfillment.

Naturally, there is Biblical support for both points of view. For those who ignore the coming judgment, Jesus of Nazareth's command not to worry in Matthew 6:24-34 provides the scriptural basis for their reaction. For those spending an inordinate amount of time looking for signs, Jesus' command to be watchful in Matthew 24:37-44 validates their approach.

This brief interpretation of what is to come, based on scriptures found both in the Gospels as well as in the books of Daniel and Revelation, falls somewhere between these two extremes.

We must preface these writings with a simple

disclosure: There is no human who knows the exact time that the world will end. Further, there is no human who knows exactly how the world will end in a general sense, for experiencing the end of the world will be both a deeply personal experience as well as a universally polarizing event which will determine the eternal fate of both individuals and communities.

Generalizations about the end times, including the one you are about to read, should be used for entertainment purposes only. Any action should be taken only after consulting the scriptures on your own and consulting with the Living God, who will gently guide all who ask Him for guidance.

That said, our limited studies of eschatology and monetary theory have led us to some inescapable conclusions that we are compelled to share in this brief volume. For those of you unfamiliar with the term, eschatology is the study of the ultimate destiny of humanity, more commonly referred to today as the "*end times*."

In order to better understand the points of view expressed in this volume, we present two facts that shape our worldview. First, that the earth was created some 5,772 years ago as of this writing, in agreement with the Jewish calendar, as well as the fact that Jesus of Nazareth, who was crucified, dead, and raised from the dead some 2000 years ago, is the Messiah and that He will return to reign on the earth at an unknown and unknowable future date.

Consequently, we accept the Bible as both an accurate historical narrative as well as a reliable guide for what is to come.

It is our prayer that you will find both comfort

EPILOGUE: ESCHATOLOGY AND MONEY: A BRIEF LOOK AT WHAT IS TO COME

and a call to action in our interpretation of what is to come. With the proper preparations, all of the peoples of the world may eagerly await the coming of the Messiah without fear and full of hope and joy.

GIVE TO CAESAR WHAT IS CAESAR'S

Jesus of Nazareth speaks with authority. As such, his words often astounded and confused those, whom in the days when he physically walked the earth nearly 2,000 years ago, had aligned both their activities and mindsets with the authority of this world, an authority which works to suppress the knowledge of the Living God.

The first passages that we will investigate are related in Matthew 22:15-22, Mark 12:14-17, and Luke 20:21-25. They focus on what appears to have been a brief verbal exchange between Jesus and a group of spies sent to ask a question of him by the religious authorities. This conversation appears to take place in the courtyard of the Second Temple in Jerusalem around the time of the Jewish Passover, which today is celebrated at the time of year that is known as Easter in the Christian tradition.

Interestingly enough, it seems that people 2,000 years ago were as eager to avoid paying taxes as they are today. In an attempt to catch Jesus advocating

EPILOGUE: ESCHATOLOGY AND MONEY: A BRIEF LOOK AT WHAT IS TO COME

for tax avoidance, the religious leaders, who wanted to get rid of Jesus, send spies to trap him in his words.

In response, Jesus not only foils their attempt at trapping him, He provides the world with a simple monetary concept with wide ranging consequences. He challenges the spies not on whether or not it is right to pay taxes, but rather on what they are using as money.

When asked whether or not it was right to pay the Roman Imperial tax, Jesus stated the obvious, "*give to Caesar what is Caesar's.*" Given that the coin used to pay the tax belonged to Caesar (the Roman Emperor) to begin with, it should be no problem to simply give it back to him when he asks for it.

The obvious yet staggering implication is that money and coinage given by an Emperor may at some point be demanded back by that Emperor, therefore it is foolish to accumulate money and coinage issued by an Emperor as a store of one's wealth.

Jesus' response cut to the heart of monetary theory by questioning not what they were doing with their money, but what they were using as money. The people's choice to use the Emperor's money had enslaved them to the Emperor in a way that no army or jail master could, and they were eager for a way out.

In those days, Emperors made a habit of declaring themselves gods and demanding allegiance. The Jews were peculiar in that they refused to recognize these imposters and instead steadfastly worshiped the Living God. However, the Jews also had become accustomed to conceding certain aspects of their allegiance to the Emperor in an effort to survive as a people.

Jesus, with a simple statement, challenged them to get off the fence, for the fence would one day be burned down and they would have to make a clear choice between ultimate allegiance to the Emperors of this world or to the One True Living God, who alone is worthy of glory and honor and praise forever and ever.

Today, circa 2012, it is customary for most people to exchange their labor for paper or digital currency issued by the Emperor. For most, it appears to be a matter of survival. Yet some 2,000 years ago, Jesus sternly warned us against this.

Why would Jesus have opinions on what we use as money? Jesus knew that a person's heart would be where his treasure was. One day, God's people would be presented with yet another ultimatum that would require them to assent to forever throwing their lot in with one of two camps, either that of the world's Imperial system, or that of The Living God.

When and how will this ultimatum present itself? What form will it take and what would be the price for holding steadfastly to The Living God? The answer to these questions had already been partially revealed to Daniel some 600 years before, and was going to be completely revealed to John on the Isle of Patmos some 70 years later.

THE VISION OF JOHN

Examining Jesus' interaction with and response to the spies' question, it is clear that He ascribed little importance and value to the coinage of Caesar. This flew in the face of what most people believed about money on a subconscious level at the time.

The unwavering faith that most people placed in the monetary system some 2,000 years ago is alive, well, and even stronger today than ever before. Yet the current monetary system, where money is debt, creates an unnatural link between human beings, a sort of mutual slave/master relationship in which each and every person within the system finds himself or herself ensnared.

How does Caesar, or his modern day counterpart, ensnare people in this system? There are generally two extraordinarily simple steps to monetary domination. First, he places his mark on the coinage. This act, as Jesus observed, makes the coins in circulation the property of Caesar. The second step is to pass a series of laws, commonly known today as legal tender laws, which obligate people to use the coinage in trade and commerce.

Jesus' words *"Give to Caesar what is Caesar's,"* therefore, may be seen as a call out of the system of Imperial coinage and tribute. If one remains in the system by accepting and using the coinage in exchange for goods and labor, they remain a slave to the Emperor and all of the money bearing his mark, which they have accumulated, belongs to Caesar.

Today, some 2,000 years after Jesus' words, most of the Western world lives in a system where not only does the modern day Caesar lay claim to their money via a mark, but also their future output by means of debts which are incurred as a necessity in the face of the declining real world value of the Imperial coinage in trade.

And yet it is only money, nothing more. Jesus stressed both private property rights and God's divine sovereignty over all property when He followed his advice to *"Give to Caesar what is Caesar's,"* with, *"and to God what is God's,"* implying that everything is God's while recognizing the right for Caesar to lay claim to all Imperial coinage via the mark.

This brings us to the second passage that we will examine in this study. The second passage relates to us a portion of the vision given to the Apostle John as he was exiled on the Isle of Patmos in the Aegean Sea circa 95 AD.

The passage, Revelation 13:14-18, taken literally, can be a source of fear amongst Christians, as it warns of a time when all people on the earth will be forced to make a seemingly permanent choice between accepting the "mark of the beast" and

EPILOGUE: ESCHATOLOGY AND MONEY: A BRIEF LOOK AT WHAT IS TO COME

"buying and selling." The worry stems from the perception that one will be forced to accept the mark, and as a consequence, presumably be forever estranged from Jesus, to be able to put bread on the table for themselves and their families. On the surface, these fears are completely understandable.

Yet in light of the coming rapture of the Church, these fears are completely unfounded.

We are of the opinion that Jesus will rapture us (those who have accepted Jesus as their savior) before the inhabitants of the earth are faced with this fateful decision. This opinion is based on the parallels between the Rapture and Jewish wedding traditions, where the bride (a metaphor for the Church of Christ) is swept away for seven days.

The parallel is that Jesus will come to sweep us away and hide us in his house (Heaven) for the seven years of the tribulation that was revealed to John in his vision (Matthew 25, Revelation 19:7-9). This interpretation is supported by everything else that Jesus said about the end of the world, and is consistent with both scriptural extremes of not worrying (Matthew 6:24-34) and being prepared (Matthew 24:37-44).

For we are not to worry that Jesus would abandon us at the time of our greatest trial. Nor should we lose vigilance in living a life pleasing to God each and every day as we eagerly await His return.

While no one knows exactly when Jesus will come, it is reasonable to expect that He will return around the time of Rosh Hashanah, the Jewish New Year. The first coming of the Messiah, Jesus, was the culmination of the Jewish Passover which occurs in the springtime. It could logically follow that the second coming of Jesus would occur during the harvest time around the Feast of Trumpets. Though we do not know the time of Jesus' return, we may know the season. Further, we are told that the feasts of the Lord are but a shadow of the things to come (Colossians 2:16-17).

If you, too, would like to share this joyful fate, we encourage you to choose today to trust Jesus. At this point, you may stop reading this study (seriously!) and begin a life of praise and service to God. What follows is meant to provide hope and encouragement to those who will accept the Living God as Lord and Savior only after the Rapture.

In the event that one chooses to decline God's loving invitation at this time and finds themselves on the earth when humanity is faced with the ultimatum to either accept the mark of the beast or to be denied access to a perceived economic necessity, namely, "buying and selling," please read on, for there will still be time to choose eternal life with God, but it will involve a seemingly difficult decision.

There is no shortage of speculation as to what form the "*mark of the beast*" will take, ranging from barcode tattoos, implanted microchips, and even to the denial of the choice to worship on Sunday. Here we do not wish to add to this mountain of speculation. Rather than focus on the substance which the mark will take, it is more important to focus on what it will mean, for at the time of the ultimatum, the choice that the people will be asked to make will be subtle and at the same time, crystal clear for all of mankind.

It is important to understand that God's enemy,

EPILOGUE: ESCHATOLOGY AND MONEY: A BRIEF LOOK
AT WHAT IS TO COME

Satan, desires to occupy the place of God in people's lives and that the obligation to worship an image and accept a mark will be his final, desperate attempt to obtain all of human worship for himself. It will be presented through a final, desperate deception, for the true nature of Satan will soon thereafter be laid bare for all to see. His nature is to lie, and his desire is nothing more than to destroy all of humanity through his lies.

It is clear that this final, desperate attempt will fail, yet it is understood that the deception will be so great that even some of those who are following Jesus may be led astray. For this reason, it is important for all those who remain after the Rapture to be aware of the nature of the choice that will be presented.

The acceptance or denial of the mark will be a choice that all those on earth will be forced to make, and it appears to be the final watershed event in human history. The choice for those living at that time will be clear to them and the consequences eternal.

The choice is the following: Will one accept the mark and throw their lot in with the world which can be seen or will one deny the mark and throw their lot in with the unseen God, and as a consequence subject themselves and their family to being ostracized from the world system to face hunger, persecution, torture, and death?

Denying the mark will likely be similar to losing title to all of one's assets and loss of access to the banking system. It will mean being shut out of the world's economic system.

The choice that each person makes at that time

will then be clear for all to see. It will symbolize either entitlement to goods, services, and protection in the world system or being cast out of it to wander the earth as Cain did

*{**Editor's Note:** Ironically, as Cain was cast out of Eden to wander the earth after murdering his brother Abel, in the narrative found in Genesis Chapter 4, it is God who sets a mark upon Cain so that none will do him harm. This same mark is promised to the servants of God mentioned in Revelation chapters 7 and 14}.*

Those who desire to throw their lot in with God at that time are then presented with the some very important questions: How long can you and your family survive without access to your assets or the banking system? Is it worth it to resist the mark and live as wanderers? Won't God understand if you take the mark and forgive even this transgression?

To the first two questions, only you can provide the answers. The Bible is clear as to the answer to the third question, and from what we read in Revelation 14:9-12, it would appear that the answer is no.

So, then, the true believers who find themselves on the earth after the Rapture are left to prepare to live outside of the system until Jesus comes for them, to keep their lamp lit until the groom comes.

But for how long? That, for those who choose to reject the mark and cling to God's promises, is the exciting part. For a brief look at Daniel reveals the answer to this final question and provides hope and comfort for all willing to throw their lot in with the Living God and eagerly await his eternal reign.

THE VISION OF DANIEL

Roughly 60 years after Jesus' interaction with the spies in which He shockingly advised them to "*give to Caesar what is Caesar's, and to God what is God's,*" the Apostle John was given a vision of the events that would transpire before Jesus returned to the earth to reign triumphantly.

Human logic would lead us to believe that a further understanding of John's vision, which gives rise to some troubling questions, would be found by examining information which became available after John shared his vision with the world. However, it is God's great delight to hide things and to watch men discover them, for it brings Him glory and further confirms His blessed sovereignty.

This study of Eschatology is no exception, for in it we find that Jesus and later John are confirming and expanding on a vision of the end times given to God's servant Daniel during the Jewish people's exile to Babylon some 600 years BEFORE Jesus came to dwell among men.

It is important to note that this is not unprecedented; in addition to the vision of Daniel regarding the end times, a vision of Jesus' first coming was given to the prophet Isaiah some 700 years prior to it happening (Isaiah 9:6-7).

John's vision, which he faithfully recorded in the book of Revelation, covers a great deal of topics and is perhaps the most widely studied book when it comes to Eschatology. Yet only by looking at the completeness of the Word of God and paying close attention to His leading can we gain a proper understanding of John's important book.

As such, it is appropriate to look back briefly at John's vision as we approach the vision of Daniel.

In this series, we are specifically concerned with only the portion of John's vision which is commonly referred to as the "*mark of the beast.*" In our review, we stated that the "*beast (i.e. satan)*" will at some point in the future demand the worship of all men through a final deception. Specifically, he will seek to ban all worship of the One True Living God and cause a statue to be set up which is described by John in Revelation 13:14. Both Jesus (Matthew 24:15, Mark 13:14) and Daniel (Daniel 9:27, 11:31) refer to this statue as the "*abomination which causes desolation.*" It is written that the beast, acting on behalf of satan, will demand that everyone on the earth render worship to the statue in direct violation of the second commandment (Deuteronomy 5:8-9).

One tactic that will be used to coerce mankind into worshiping the dead statue instead of the One True Living God will be to require mankind to accept a "*mark*" on their physical body in order to be able to buy and sell. The worship of the statue in

EPILOGUE: ESCHATOLOGY AND MONEY: A BRIEF LOOK AT WHAT IS TO COME

some form will be required in order to receive the mark.

The choice to accept or deny this mark will be the watershed moment for the inhabitants of the earth at that time. They will be forced to choose to either throw their lot in with satan, whose kingdom is being destroyed forever, or the One True Living God, whose Kingdom is already established for eternity.

On paper, the choice between kingdoms is obvious. Logically, one should quickly choose to live in the Kingdom of God. However, given the deception that satan constantly employs in an attempt to manipulate mankind, a measure of perseverance will be required.

Just how much perseverance are we talking about? The prospect of losing title to all of their possessions and not being able to buy or sell may be too much for even self professed Christians to bear, and many, faced with the choice to continue their way of life within the system or to presumably wander the earth as Cain did, may be tricked into capitulating to Satan's tactic and accepting the mark.

Remember, the Rapture will occur before any of the tribulations, including the dreaded choice of whether or not to accept the "*mark of the beast*," takes place. Therefore, if the end times which John writes of seem like too much to bear (as it is for us,) we implore you to begin trusting Jesus today. These words are meant to provide hope and encouragement to those who will accept the Living God as Lord and Savior only after the rapture.

Those who are living on the earth during the

perilous days to come, the third and final passage which we will consider is intended to give them a measure of hope, as well as the timeframe which one must be prepared to endure, the period of time for which perseverance will be required.

The vision of Daniel regarding the end times, related in the book of Daniel, Chapter 12, taken together with the vision of John in Revelation gives us the specific time frame that the "*mark of the beast*" will be required to be used for buying and selling within the earth's system.

It is clear from John's vision that the imposition of the mark will coincide with the erection of the statue which God calls the "*abomination which causes desolation.*" Therefore, according to Daniel 12:11-12, the time frame from the beginning of the tribulations until the time that the decision to accept or reject the mark is presented to all of those on the earth at that time, will be 1,290 days, or approximately 3 years and 6 months.

If one finds him or herself on the earth at this time, we advise you to use those 1,290 days to prepare at least 45 days of rations.

Why 45 days? Because 45 days is the period of time which one will have to refrain from buying or selling if they desire to accept Jesus and reject the mark of the beast. As it is related in Daniel 12:12:

"Blessed is the one who waits for and reaches the end of 1,335 days."

Again, 45 days is all one will have to refrain from buying or selling as a consequence of wisely rejecting the mark of the beast. During this

EPILOGUE: ESCHATOLOGY AND MONEY: A BRIEF LOOK AT WHAT IS TO COME

extremely short period of time, the beast will appear to have complete control over the monetary realm. Those who have refused to accept the mark will be ridiculed and likely pursued and persecuted unto death.

Then, after 45 days, the fraudulent monetary and religious system that the beast has attempted to impose on the earth will utterly and completely collapse, and all of the earth will fall into a deeper tribulation as a result. However, it is clear from Daniel's vision that those who refused to accept the mark of the beast will be blessed!

Hallelujah!

45 days may seem like a long time to wander the earth as Cain did, but with the proper preparations, all of the peoples of the world who remain after the rapture and endure the coming tribulation may eagerly await the coming of Jesus without fear and full of hope.

They will not roam alone, as Cain did, but will band together to ensure that not one is lost as they eagerly await the return of their Lord and Savior, our Lord and Savior, the world's Lord and Savior, Jesus Christ.

CONCLUSION AND ENCOURAGEMENT

In this brief but necessary excursion into the wild world of Eschatology, we have endeavored to bring to your attention what one can expect in the Monetary Realm as the world comes to an end.

We are not predicting when the world will come to an end, for only God alone can determine this, rather, we are sharing our interpretation of what will take place regarding man's relationship to his money and possessions as the inevitable trials and tribulations which will take place begin to unfold.

We are aware that this is but one of many interpretations of the events surrounding the end times, yet it is our prayer that you will find both comfort and a call to action in our interpretation of what is to come.

God is faithful and will quickly answer honest and earnest prayer. We encourage everyone to study the Bible and to seek God in order to develop their own understanding of what is to happen and

EPILOGUE: ESCHATOLOGY AND MONEY: A BRIEF LOOK AT WHAT IS TO COME

what they are to do as His Kingdom comes.

Peace and blessings in the Name of our Lord Jesus Christ to all who read these words. May you be encouraged and emboldened in your faith, and may we be found faithful to the Lord today and always.

AFTERWORD: THE CHARGE

These varied volumes have grown as fruit of a journey of discovery that has lasted just over ten years. The fruit is now ripe and the harvest is near. Are you, *"deer" (sic)* reader, the one of a million souls who will hear the call and take the actions, or inactions, as it were, necessary to turn back the clock of centralized planning and climate change before it is too late?

If you have successfully made it through these volumes without your blood boiling over in disaccord, chances are that you the one in a million; otherwise known as a peacemaker. As a peacemaker, armed with nothing more than boundless energy and nimble wit, you will make history, and these volumes, along with the resources bequeathed to us by fellow peacemakers throughout the ages, will help keep the flame of true freedom alive for generations to come.

For the future belongs not to those who would plan it and take it by force, but to those who will set

EPILOGUE: ESCHATOLOGY AND MONEY: A BRIEF LOOK AT WHAT IS TO COME

it free by working to embrace The Better Way, a perfect anarchy where there is only one rule, which is emblazoned on every heart:

"Love your neighbor as you love yourself"

INTERIOR COVER CREDITS

PROLOGUE

Cover design by Tatiana Wilcox

VOLUME I

Cover design by David Mint at WDesign

Adaptation of the painting "*Joseph and His Brethren Welcomed by Pharaoh,*" watercolor by French painter James Tissot, ca. 1900 (b.1836 d.1902)

VOLUME II

Cover design by David Mint at WDesign.

Adaptation of a coin struck by David Mint at the Casa de la Moneda in Potosí, Bolivia, circa 2009

INTERIOR DESIGN CREDITS

VOLUME III

Cover design by David Mint at WDesign

Adaptation of a photograph taken by David Mint of a collection of Canadian, Bolivian, and freely minted coins, circa 2013

VOLUME IV

Cover design by David Mint at WDesign
Adaptation of a stylized anarchy symbol by David Mint

VOLUME V

Cover design by David Mint at WDesign

Adaptation of a portrait of Karl Marx taken before August 24, 1875 from the International Institute of Social History in Amsterdam beside a photograph taken by Michael Greene of the Atlas sculpture by Lee Lawrie located in New York City superimposed over a representation of both the Anarcho-Capitalist flag and the flag of the Soviet Union.

VOLUME VI

Cover design by David Mint at WDesign

Adaptation of the painting *"Ritratto di fra' Luca*

Pacioli con un allievo (Guidobaldo da Montefeltro?)," (Portrait of Franciscan Luca Pacioli with a Student (perhaps Guidobaldo of Montefeltro, Duke of Urbino, a fervent scholar to whom Pacioli's Summa was dedicated). tempera on panel likely painted by either Italian Renaissance artist Jacopo de'Barbari, though the portrait has also been attributed to Leonardo da Vinci, ca. 1500 (b.1470? d.1516?)

VOLUME VII

Cover design by David Mint at WDesign

Adaptation of *American Gothic*, a painting created in 1930 by American Grant Wood (b.1891 - d.1942), Oil on Beaver Board

EPILOGUE

Cover design by Tatiana Wilcox at WDesign

Adaptation of an 15th century woodcut by Albrecht Dürer (1471 - 1528), *The Revelation of St John: The Four Riders of the Apocalypse*, created in Nuremberg between 1497-98. Original image source: http://www.wga.hu/html/d/durer/2/12/2apocaly/index.html {{PD}}.

ABOUT THE AUTHOR

David is happily married with two children and lives in Portland, Oregon where he has pondered monetary theory and other less pressing but infinitely more entertaining matters since 2006. He has travelled extensively in the United States and has resided in Nebraska, Colorado, Oregon, Spain, and Bolivia.

He has a Bachelors degree in Business Administration from Colorado State University and an MBA from the Universitat de Barcelona, Spain with over 18 years of experience in Accounting, Finance, Treasury, and Information Systems Consulting positions both in the United States and Spain

He is the creator of The Mint, which presents fresh ideas on Economics, Monetary Theory, and Politics. You can read The Mint at http://www.davidmint.com and you may contact him at davidminteconomics@gmail.com.

www.ingramcontent.com/pod-product-compliance
Lightning Source LLC
Chambersburg PA
CBHW051623170526
45167CB00001B/33